RECLAIM
YOUR SCHOOL

TEN STRATEGIES TO PRACTICALLY AND LEGALLY EVANGELIZE YOUR SCHOOL

BRAD & SUSANNE DACUS

PACIFIC JUSTICE
INSTITUTE

Reclaim Your School
by Brad & Susanne Dacus

Copyright © Pacific Justice Institute
Administered in the United States by Pacific Justice Institute

Printing May 2002
Second Edition August 2004
Third Edition February 2007

EDITED BY
Carolyn Caforio
Lisa Ebbesen
Jodi Harris
Tiffaney Lyda
Kevin Snider
Morgan Vetter

TYPESET BY
Alpha Graphics – Fresno

PRINTED IN THE UNITED STATES BY
BookPrintingRevolution.com - Minneapolis, MN

COVER DESIGN BY
Jenni Wheeler

PRODUCTION AND DISTRIBUTION BY
Pacific Justice Institute
P.O. Box 276600
Sacramento, CA 95827
Ph. (916) 857-6900
(888) 305-9129
Fax (916) 857-6902
Web Site – www.pacificjustice.org

ENDORSEMENTS
Pacific Justice Institute

"Living in times, as we do now, where there is a general assault on all vestiges and manifestations of faith and religion in our public life… I think that we must see with clarity the importance – but also the encouraging significance – of the Pacific Justice Institute and of those who dedicate their time and energy to the great work being done here. In the context of our constitutional way of life, I can think of no work under the law that is more important than the work they are doing – and I thank God for them."

Ambassador Alan Keyes
Quoted from the Christian Times Today, June 2004

"Your hard work defending civil liberties, including your invaluable services to those who could not otherwise afford legal assistance, will help to restore reverence for our state and nation. I am confident Pacific Justice Institute will be successful in carrying out this important mission."

Congressman Dan Lungren
Former Attorney General, California

"Pacific Justice Institute's president, attorney Brad Dacus, has established a distinguished track record throughout the West as an effective advocate for countless individuals and religious organizations needing first rate legal assistance. In addition, I have had the pleasure of hearing Mr. Dacus speak, and I found him to be a very inspiring and motivational speaker, combining sincere conviction with practical application of the law. I expect the Pacific Justice Institute to play a valuable role in defending civil liberties well into the next century. I therefore offer my wholehearted support for this exceptional organization."

Edwin Meese, Chairman
Pacific Justice Institute Advisory Board
Former Attorney General, United States of America

"I'm excited to see how God is using this ministry to bless churches and congregations. Mr. Dacus was a very inspiring and motivational speaker to my congregation. I offer my wholehearted support."

Pastor Daniel Henderson
Arcade Baptist Church
Sacramento, California

"Pacific Justice Institute is the only organization of its kind in California having a broad network of attorneys willing to represent individuals and religious institutions without charge."

Raymond N. Haynes
Former State Senator, California

ENDORSEMENTS
Reclaim Your School

"This book could revolutionize every high school campus in America."

Pastor Larry DiSimone
Calvary Chapel of the Canyons
Silverado Canyon, California

"Pacific Justice Institute has proven to be a valuable ministry for churches wishing to reach out to their community. This book is a natural continuation of that ministry, and our church is excited to support their work."

Pastor Rick Cole
Capital Christian Center
Sacramento, California

"I have seen firsthand and have been very impressed with how the Pacific Justice Institute both helps school districts and keeps them in line when necessary."

Jim Gibson
School Board Member
Oceanside, California

"This book has the potential to transform public schools everywhere. Brad and Susanne Dacus skillfully show us how to passionately and legally impact public schools for the Gospel. I am strongly encouraging every parent in our church to read this book! Pastors everywhere, including those that work with children and youth, need to own Reclaim Your School!"

Pastor Rick Stedman
Adventure Christian Church
Roseville, California

"The opportunities for teachers to share their faith in public schools are greater than I thought. This book will open up the eyes of many teachers who thought their hands were tied when it came to living out their Christian faith. I hope teachers everywhere, in elementary, junior high and high schools, read this book with vision and excitement!"

Christy Kedulich
Teacher
Walnut, California

"In a day when Christians are failing to stand up for Christ in the public school system because of fear or ignorance, Brad and Susanne Dacus demonstrate how you can biblically, legally, and courageously evangelize your school for the glory of God. This book is long overdue."

Pastor Rich Sherman
Sunrise Community Church
Fair Oaks, California

DEDICATION

This book is dedicated to our precious son and daughter,
Austin Bradley Dacus and Amy Susanne Dacus.

Our prayer for them is that they would eventually desire to share their
faith out of an overwhelming love for the Lord . . .
and still have the freedom to do so.

This book also recognizes the invaluable work of
John W. Whitehead,
the founder of the modern religious freedom movement.

ACKNOWLEDGEMENTS

A book like this is only possible with the help of others. There are many people whom we would like to thank for making this book a reality.

We owe a special debt to those who are a part of the Pacific Justice Institute team. It is because of your support and prayers that we were able to get this book project off the ground.

Despite numerous roles and responsibilities, Tiffaney Lyda, great friend and English Professor at Hope International University, took the time to edit this book project. Thanks, Tiffaney, for your gentle, yet truthful criticism. Your close friendship is invaluable.

Thanks to James Bourbeau for designing our wonderful book cover. Without his expertise we could not have done it!

Thanks to Jodi Harris and Lisa Ebbesen for participating in the editing process.

Thanks to Rick Stedman for taking the time to make valuable recommendations at the final stages of this project.

Beginning this first book project seemed overwhelming at first. Thanks to Kathleen McNama (Susanne's sister) for reading our very first draft and for giving us important guidance and encouragement.

A big thank you to Morgan Vetter. Morgan, this book literally could not have happened without your editorial skills, and more importantly, your willingness to use your skills to honor God. We are so grateful.

Finally, thanks to God who provided the purpose and passion for the authors to write this book.

PREFACE

"Is that legal?" "Can we do that?" "What can I do to share God in my public school?" "How can I make that actually happen?" "How can I know that I am doing what God really wants me to do on campus?" We have heard these questions numerous times on our travels throughout the country for speaking engagements. While I enjoy such opportunities, my goal for quite some time has been to answer these questions much more thoroughly and for a much larger audience. God, in his providence, made this goal possible several years ago when I took Susanne to be my wife. While I have ten years of legal experience answering these questions as a lawyer, Susanne has ten years of practical experience answering these questions as a youth minister. This combination has created a unique book that is informative, yet interesting and practical for a wide range of people with a genuine heart to make a difference.

While Pacific Justice Institute works diligently to defend the religious freedom of all people, our personal perspective as authors is based on our Christian faith. Consequently, it is from this perspective that this book is written. My vision is that this book will be used throughout the country to reclaim the spiritual void existing in public education.

Brad W. Dacus, Esq.

CONTENTS

DO YOU GET THE PICTURE?
What Evangelism Means in Everyday Life

"I evangelize because I was once evangelized."
John Guest

"Can we afford to be selfish with the gospel, when there is overwhelming evidence that the majority of people are hungry for God?"
Bill Bright

We had only been married a few months when we were on a flight to San Diego where Brad was scheduled to speak. Brad was in the aisle seat, I was in the middle seat, and a woman —probably in her mid-twenties— had the window seat. While experiencing some sudden and violent turbulence, Brad leaned forward past me, looked at the woman seated next to the window and said, "If you died today, do you know what would happen to you?" Then he ever so calmly leaned back in his seat, leaving me with a wide-eyed and confused young woman. This began a good discussion about her life, work and beliefs. I found out she was in the military, which can be a very lonely occupation. My brother-in-law was in the military for ten years and shared how it can be a lonely place, especially if you are single and far from home. From speaking with this young woman, I found out that she was both single and far from home. We had an interesting talk that ended up lasting the rest of the flight. I asked if she had a Bible and she said she did not. I ended up giving her my Bible right before we landed and encouraged her to begin reading the book of John. I have to admit that I still miss that Bible, but Brad bought me a new one for my birthday.

That was one of our first evangelism experiences together as a married couple. Before we were married, most of our discussions with strangers, prompted by Brad, of course, began with his telling strangers about our pledge to be sexually abstinent until marriage. Now that we are married, many of our discussions with strangers begin with our enjoyment of being married. Both of those subjects open up doors to speak with people of all ages. Regarding these evangelism opportunities, one of Brad's personal favorites is to speak to young people while they are out on dates. He usually asks the young couple if they are dating and then he shares with them the advantage of abstaining from sex until marriage. These subjects often, if not always, lead us to a discussion of Christ's work in our lives and the joy, hope, and peace we have in Him.

What Does Evangelism Mean to You?

John Guest, an evangelist and speaker, once said while speaking at a Youth Specialties Youth Worker Conference, "I evangelize because I was once evangelized." I attended this conference in the early and middle 1990's in San Diego at the Town and Country Hotel. I was sitting with my youth worker friends and, as usual, we were anticipating an interesting and motivating afternoon speaker. Guest opened his message with that phrase, and it has stuck with me ever since. *"I evangelize because I was once evangelized."* This statement powerfully communicates that we can share our faith solely because someone once shared his or her faith with us. We ought to also respond to what Christ did on the cross for us. Christ's love compels us to share Him with others. **Someone's choice to share the gospel with us enables us to share that love with others.**

The word "evangelism" provokes a variety of emotions in Christians. A person's reaction to the word "evangelism" often depends on his or her personality, relationship with God, and biblical training. To which one of these emotional reactions can you relate?

- Just the *thought* of sharing my faith with another makes my palms sweat and my heart beat faster.

- The idea of sharing my faith is met with apathy and unconcern.

- Telling others about the transforming work of Christ in my life is an exciting and welcoming prospect.

- Evangelism is a bit intimidating to me, but I would have more confidence if I could learn more about how to share my faith.

Before you continue reading, take a moment to consider which person you are. One or more of these reactions probably describes you. After deciding which of these descriptions fits you, read on!

What If I Am Afraid To Share My Faith?

If you are the one whose knees start shaking at the mere thought of evangelism, just remember, sharing your faith is not meant to be an experience *full of stress* but an experience *full of faith!* In fact, evangelism is much like telling a story. Better than that, it is really telling a story about yourself. Part of your fear may be a result of your shy and timid personality. As a child, I too was very shy and timid. As an introvert, even now I definitely speak from experience when I say it can be difficult or intimidating to share my faith. However, I have found that in a small group or one-on-one situation, many people can be a bit shy until they are asked a question about their life or about experiences they have had. A simple question or the right button pushed can usually turn timid people into talkative ones. In the same way, it may be out of your comfort zone to begin conversations about your faith with people, but remember, *sharing your faith begins with sharing your life.*

Think about this. What kind of person is most excited about sharing his or her faith? Often the new Christians we see are jumping in with both feet, ready to share their faith without realizing they may not have all the answers. They are so excited about sharing what Christ has done in their lives they do not stop to worry about what they do not know because they are so excited about what they do know. It is not until later that Christians develop inhibitions about sharing their faith. New Christians often respond out of the emotion of their newfound faith and relationship with God. One who has been a Christian for a long time can become jaded or take for granted that relationship and forget that others need and desire to know the Lord. However, we know Christ did not make it an option to evangelize—He commanded it.

One effective way of sharing your faith is by building relationships with others. Remember, you do not have to plunge into the four spiritual laws with someone during your lunch break at school. You can simply talk to a fellow student, a fellow teacher, or your child's teacher about mutual interests you both may have. As you continue in your discussion and possibly develop a friendship, the subject of your faith will be much easier and much more natural to discuss. Even if you consider yourself shy, God may be calling you to share with a stranger or someone you do not know very well at your school. This may be an intimidating thought, but remember that "….God did not give us a spirit of timidity, but a spirit of power, of love and of self-discipline."[1] Therefore, rely on God for His power and leading when He is calling you to share Him with someone—that, by the way, He does at all times.

It is also important to remember that sharing your faith can be done in a variety of ways. For purposes of this book we are limiting our evangelism strategies to the public school system. Students have shared their faith in book reports and school projects. Parents have shared their faith with their children's teachers. Youth pastors have helped their youth begin Christian clubs on campus. Teachers have volunteered to be sponsors of those Christian clubs. These are just a few of the many ways in which individuals can effectively and legally share their faith on campus in a public school. As you continue to read, you will learn a variety of ways to share your faith at your school, whether you are a student, an administrator, a teacher, a pastor, or a parent. Two of the chapters in this book address how to share the gospel and why and how to develop your personal testimony of how you came to Christ. While it may sound intimidating, it is really much simpler than you would think. We sincerely hope that reading this book will calm your heart and give you the encouragement you need to take that step of faith to share your faith.

What If I Am Apathetic About Sharing My Faith?

For those of you who greet the idea of evangelism with apathy and unconcern, we suggest that you read your Bible. Numerous verses not only encourage, but also command us to share our faith. At this time, we will focus on only a few.

> *"But in your hearts set apart Christ as Lord. Always*
> *be prepared to give an answer to everyone who*
> *asks you to give the reason for the hope that you have.*
> *But do this with gentleness and respect."* [2]

If we have a living faith in Christ and a living hope in Him, we will also have a living testimony for Him. That living testimony will be shown in a number of ways at school, through our example, our lifestyle, and our willingness to speak about Christ when He puts it on our heart to do so. If you are a believer, the Holy Spirit is working in you right now, and if you listen to the Holy Spirit, you will find Him prodding you to share your faith with friends, family, and sometimes even strangers.

When Paul wrote to the church from prison he said, *"So do not be ashamed to testify about our Lord..."*[3] Neither should we, as Christians today, be ashamed to testify about our Lord. The early church knew that the consequences of sharing their faith were great, much greater consequences than we deal with today. In that day Christians were persecuted, tortured, imprisoned, and put to death for their faith. We may face that some time in the future, but right now the persecution we find people facing is possible rejection from others, potential job loss, or even harassment at school or work. This harassment may take the form of simply being laughed at or other ways of humiliation may be used. Our legal system does provide protection for Christians who share their faith legally at school and in the workplace. Some of these provisions will be addressed in this book. Remember you still may experience consequences such as humiliation or rejection; however, you will not have a criminal record just for sharing your faith! While we do not want to minimize these possible consequences, none can compare to what the early church experienced. How easy it would have been for them to stay quiet about their faith. How easy it would have been to be a "closet" Christian and not take the chance of sharing the good news of Christ with others. If anyone had a reason to hold back, they did. But Paul told them not to hold back. He exhorted the church not to be ashamed to testify, or tell, others about Christ. Shouldn't we be compelled to do the same?

> *"For the love of Christ controls us, having concluded this, that one died for all, therefore all died. And he died for all, that they who live should no longer live for themselves, but for Him who died and rose again on their behalf."*[4]

It is the love of Christ that controls us, not the law. If you are jaded or have a hardened heart about the love of Christ, consider what Christ did on the cross for you. Remember, as Charles Sheldon stated so emotionally,

"*. . . the steps of Him who trod the way with groans and tears and sobs of anguish for a lost humanity; who sweat, as it were, great drops of blood, who cried out on the unreared cross, 'My God, my God, why hast thou forsaken me?'*"[5] It is that tremendous and unending love that ought to compel us to share with others.

God uses prayer to soften our hearts. He uses prayer to help us see others as He sees them, and love others as He loves them. Choose to pray for just two or three people around you who do not know the Lord.

Take some proactive steps to discover why and how your heart can be changed. First, lift up your heart to God in prayer. Not a two-second prayer said right now, but take time daily to lift up your indifferent heart to God and ask Him to transform it. Pray that He might make the reality of judgment, heaven, and hell real to you so you can see without a doubt the consequences of others' belief and disbelief in God. Pray that He will open your eyes to people around you who are faced with questions while you have the answer. Second, talk to one of your pastors about your lack of desire to share your faith. Young people, approach your youth pastor or one of your adult leaders. Adults, approach one of your leaders, elders, or pastors. Let them know you are not compelled to share your faith and want to know if they have any suggestions for you. Third, get involved in a small group that develops personal growth, openness, and accountability, or take an evangelism class so you can open your eyes to a lost and dying world.

What If I Am Already Active and Excited About Sharing My Faith?

For those of you who relish the idea of sharing your faith in any and all possible ways, have we got a book for you! This book will energize you even further and motivate you to evangelize on your public school campus in ways you may have never realized. Do we have an exhaustive list of how to creatively evangelize in public schools? Let me put it this way: There are as many different ideas as there are people in the world. You will find some interesting stories in this book demonstrating how creative you can be when you evangelize at school. We want the ideas in this book to act as a springboard for you. We want it to motivate you and activate your imagination so that you too can come up with new, exciting, and legal ways to share your faith to a lost and dying people, many of whom can be found in the public school system.

1

ARE YOU READY?
Rising to the Challenge of Sharing Your Faith

*"Here's the great evangelical disaster–the failure
of the evangelical world to stand for truth
as truth. There is only one word for this
–namely accommodation."*
Francis Schaeffer

The Pacific Justice Institute once represented a church in Petaluma, California, that was told they could not build a youth center unless they agreed to have the center *and* the rest of the church closed by 8:00 p.m. most nights of the week. This requirement was in spite of the fact that a nearby grocery store selling liquor was open until 1:00 in the morning and provided an unsavory place for youth to hang out. So what's a church to do? That is the question this church, and the numerous other churches that Pacific Justice Institute typically helps at any given time, had to ask.

The Christian's Response to Rights and Freedom

It is amazing to read American history and to read about the freedom and liberty that so many people value and embrace. That freedom is obviously important to us as Americans, but it should mean even more to us as Christians. Just like that church in Northern California, we will be faced with challenges as we go forth with our message of truth and faith. Christians will often be challenged when sharing their faith. Whether at work, in the community, with friends, on a sidewalk, or at school, you may face many challenges and opposition to your Christian faith.

When challenged, Christians often have one of two responses. First there is what I like to call the doormat or Father Mulcahy response. If you remember, Father Mulcahy was a character on an old television sitcom called M*A*S*H. This character never wanted to offend anyone, and if necessary, even *concealed* his faith in order to make people happy and not rock the boat. That type of person, in response to a challenge, says, "Oh well, that's okay. I don't want to offend anyone. I may have a right to say or do this, but I don't want to ruffle any feathers. I'll stop sharing and go away." This response is also sometimes called the martyrdom syndrome. As soon as that individual is faced with persecution, he accepts it, stops what he is doing and goes away.

The other response Christians have is to loudly shout about their rights. Their response might go something like this: "Oh yeah, I'll show them. They can't stop me from preaching about the love of Jesus. I'm gonna sue so they'll never forget . . .!" Well, you get the idea. Some people can get so excited and adamant about their rights they forget about sharing the love of Jesus.

So, what does this mean? Should we step back and give in when faced with challenges to our faith? Or is it more important that we hold onto our rights loudly and boldly? What is the correct response when faced with challenges to our faith? What should that church mentioned in the beginning of this chapter do? We need to look at our playbook, or our reference guide. What is the reference guide that has the answers to questions we have? It is the Bible, and if we stick to the Bible, we are safe.

Our reference point should *always* be the scriptures. That is one of many things Susanne learned from her pastor at Good Shepherd's Bible Fellowship formerly in Rowland Heights, California. Whenever Pastor Jim Richardson was asked a question or was asked for an opinion, he would always, without fail, refer to the Word of God or open it up to see what God had to say on the matter. This may sound obvious to you, but many pastors and Christians fail to do this. They would much rather rely on books written by men or the psychology they learned in school or, worse yet, public opinion. I am not saying that books are not a valuable source; however, they are to be used *in addition* to the Word of God. The Word of God must always come first as a reference. If a book ever contradicts the Bible, the Bible wins. So let's consult the Scriptures to see how Paul responded when his rights were about to be trampled on.

Paul's Response when Challenged

As we read in Acts 22, Paul is in the hot seat. He has shared the truth of the gospel, and all of Jerusalem is in an uproar. (As a side note, I want this to be a reminder and an encouragement that just because one does not get a rousing response, this does not mean that one is not called to preach the Gospel.) In Acts 22:22-25, Paul's preaching of the Gospel was met with much anger, but there is no doubt of his calling to preach. Because it is the version most familiar to me, I used the New American Standard version of the Bible for this section of the book. To read about the crowd's reaction to Paul, verse 22 is the best place to start.

> *"And they listened to him up to this statement, and then they raised their voices and said, 'Away with such a fellow from the earth, for he should not be allowed to live!' And as they were crying out and throwing dust into the air, the commander ordered him to be brought into the barracks, stating that he should be examined by scourging so that he might find out the reason why they were shouting against him that way."*

Not exactly the kind of response one wants when preaching the gospel, is it? Things are not looking good for Paul here. What is he to do? He is definitely in the minority, about to be beaten and possibly killed for sharing the truth of the gospel. Let's read on to see what happens.

> *"And when they stretched him out with thongs, Paul said to the Centurion who was standing by, 'Is it lawful for you to scourge a man who is a Roman and uncondemned?'"*

Paul is laying claim to his rights of due process under the law! And he does so in the least offensive way possible, by asking a question. Why does he do this? He does it because he regarded every person as a potential follower of Jesus Christ. Although he could have, Paul did not want to declare his rights in a loud and possibly offensive way that might turn away the soldiers who were threatening to beat him. Paul spoke with the love of Christ, *yet he still knew he had rights because of his God-given citizenship, and he chose to use those rights for the sake of the gospel.* If you read on in Acts, you will read that while Paul was arrested more than once, this time he was let go because of the declaration of his citizenship.

The Story of a Church that Stood for Faith

We ought to respond the same way that Paul did when our rights are threatened. Remember the church in Petaluma, California I spoke about in the beginning of this chapter? Let me review it for you. The church wanted to build a center for the youth in the church and the community to provide an alternative to the streets and grocery store selling liquor a couple of blocks away. To any logical and reasonable person this sounds like a good idea. Yet the city planning commission wanted to restrict the time of the youth center by closing it by 8:00 p.m. most nights of the week. They also applied this time curfew to the rest of the church for good measure. To add insult to injury, the planning commission was concerned about too many wedding ceremonies. (Trust us. Too many wedding ceremonies are not a problem in this part of the country.) So, the church contacted us at the Pacific Justice Institute.

Our legal team drafted a legal opinion letter for the city council meeting, and we attended that meeting where I had the opportunity to testify about the constitutional freedoms that were being trampled on by the insistence of these conditions. That evening as we approached the building where the city council was meeting, we could see a number of people. In fact, the seats were filled with church members, *and pastors and members of other churches!* They were beginning to pull out extra chairs, and by the time the meeting started, the people were spilling out of the building. It was exciting and encouraging to see so many people from that church and others declaring their rights. It is important to mention that the people attending were determined to claim their rights, yet they did so in a peaceful manner. It can be easy to declare our rights emphatically while forgetting that our ultimate goal is to be a witness for Christ. The people who attended this city council meeting achieved both. What I thought might turn out to be a boring meeting was actually quite exciting and ended much later than originally planned. At the end of it all, the city council completely reversed the planning commission's outrageous restrictions.

It is important that these church members did take a stand for their constitutional rights. In fact, one of the members from another church passionately stated, "Our concern is not for this church alone. If you can restrict them in this way, which one of us is next?"

This church could have simply cowered and accepted the planning commission's original conditions. But they didn't. They took a stand for their constitutional rights in the most logical and peaceful way possible. They did not confront in an offensive manner, but they did claim their rights in a reasonable manner—just as Paul did. It is great to see so many churches taking a stand for the gospel in this country. If they do not choose to take a stand now, it is a downward slide, and they will end up with more and more rights being taken away. This church is just one of many examples we will be sharing in this book about those who have stood up for their faith in a loving, Christ-like manner.

Paul Continues to Take a Stand

The case we read about in Acts 22 is not the only example of Paul's stance for his rights as a Roman citizen. In Acts 25, Paul is on trial before Festus, once again, for sharing the truth of the gospel. This is what Paul says in the first part of verse eleven:

"If then I am a wrongdoer, and have committed
anything worthy of death, I do not refuse to die;"

(As a side note, Paul has just said that if he has done anything worthy of death he will not refuse to die. Paul is willing to take the consequences if he has done something wrong. As Christians and citizens we ought to be willing to do as Paul did. If we do something wrong, God will indeed forgive us; however, we must accept the earthly consequences, just as Paul was willing to do. Although, remember, he has done nothing wrong.) Let's continue with the second half of verse eleven:

"but if none of those things is true of which these
men accuse me, no one can hand me over to them.
I appeal to Caesar."

Translated today: "I appeal to the United States Supreme Court!" That is essentially what Paul was doing when he appealed to the high-

11

est court in the land. In the same way, standing up for our constitutional rights is what we should be willing and ready to do even if it means taking the issue all the way to the Supreme Court. Paul was not "rights" driven. Through reading Scripture, I am sure Paul's goal in life was to be a witness for Christ. He was not attempting to set new case law precedents through continual litigation. In fact, one can find in Scripture that Paul was just as willing to relinquish his rights for the sake of the Gospel. Paul, however, also laid claim to his rights more than once, in a peaceful and reasonable manner, for the sake of Christ and the Gospel.

On one occasion, an angry Christian called my office wanting to "show them" (his opposition) by evangelizing. By the tone in his voice, it became obvious he had become so consumed with his "rights" that he forgot the message of Christ's love. The bottom line: Whether we lay claim to or relinquish our rights, let it be done for the glory of Christ.

Are You Willing to Take a Stand?

People often ask me if I ever become depressed because our ministry has to deal with so many important and emotional issues. I have to be instantly aware of events in our society and often witness firsthand the slippery slope of immorality that we appear to be experiencing. While I do find the cases involving innocent children most difficult to deal with (I tend to be most emotional over these cases), I find great hope in the Lord, knowing that nothing takes God by surprise. I also know that God is in control, His Word will come to pass, and in the end the Lord will win the battle. There are times, however, when I have been quite frustrated. Those times come when I see a wrong committed, yet no parent or individual is willing to take a stand for what is right.

In Central California, there was a high school English teacher who taught her students a little bit more than grammar and literature. She also taught her impressionable, young students how to make fake IDs or identification to get into adult bookstores, how to smuggle alcohol onto campus, and where to find her favorite nude beaches, just to name a few of her streetwise lessons. In a daily journaling exercise that was part of their grade, the students were reportedly instructed to address the question, "If you could murder anyone, who would it be, and how would you do it?" This was highly inappropriate behavior on the part of this teacher. How many parents do you think took a stand against this wrongdoing? *If you guessed one set of parents,* you're right. Only one set of parents was disturbed enough to make over a dozen complaints to a variety of school officials and administrators. Nothing came of these complaints, and the father was fed up with the inaction. He called the Pacific Justice Institute and spoke with us. An affiliate attorney, volunteering his time for the Pacific Justice Institute, took on this case and demanded an investigation. Eight of the nine charges were proven, and the teacher was fired. It took only one set of parents to make a difference in the lives of hundreds of students.

Entertainment or Indoctrination?

Not long ago, we found out a drama group promoting alternative lifestyles, such as homosexuality, was putting on dramatic presentations in elementary schools. I called the theatrical director of the Los Angeles Unified School District to find out more. She told me that over one hundred of these drama presentations had taken place. These presentations were not just for the entertainment of children; rather, they were obviously put on to indoctrinate young children about the homosexual lifestyle. This pro-homosexual drama group moved on to some Orange County school districts. A teacher from one of those districts called Pacific Justice Institute to inform us of what was happening. The problem? The teacher was too scared to give his name or the name of his school. Fortunately, at the same time this drama group was out "preaching their word," so were we. God has greatly blessed our ministry and provided the opportunity for me to be on many radio stations. I had the opportunity to put the word out about this drama group on Duffy and Company, a radio program that used to be on KKLA, a large radio station servicing Los Angeles and Orange County. I let the listeners know that all we needed was one parent to take a stand for the rights of parents over their children. Can you guess the number of parents and/or teachers that called us to take a stand? If you guessed none, you would be right again. The Pacific Justice Institute received no calls from concerned parents or teachers as a result of those requests. I have to admit this was very disconcerting, and the Institute had to wait several months before hearing from parents in other schools who were dealing with the same problems.

In this book you will read about the action Pacific Justice Institute is taking to prevent this usurpation of parental rights from taking place in other schools. A lot of this action takes place in a courtroom, which is important for setting good case law for future generations. Some groups talk about problems and make many people aware of the problems in our schools and society at large. However, even though PJI makes people aware of what is occurring, we are known more for taking action. We can talk all we want about the problems, but unless we fight in the courtroom and fight for each individual's freedom, we will witness a growing sense of despair with lots of talk and little action. I like to relate this concept to the Civil Rights Act of 1964. It was right that laws were passed giving equality to all people including African Americans; however, if someone did not fight every time someone's rights were not respected, what would have come of those laws? We can ignore the laws that exist, or we can stand up and fight for what is right. Standing up for what is right, for justice, and for truth is what the Pacific Justice Institute is all about. The Constitution and other laws proclaim freedom for faith and family. *Pacific Justice Institute fights to preserve it.*

Taking a Stand . . . in Kindergarten?

Believe it or not, even kindergarteners have to deal with religious discrimination. One student brought in his favorite book for his mother to read aloud during story time at his school. But when the boy proudly announced to the class that he wanted to share the story of "Jonah," his teacher informed him in front of the other students that his choice was unacceptable because his book contained the word "God." The young student's parents called the Pacific Justice Institute to see if the teacher was wrong in denying their son's right to share this particular story. One of our attorneys assured the parents of their son's rights, (see App. 3) and then called the principal to question this school "policy." Within one day, the principal contacted the family with a sincere apology informing the family that the school does have a policy in place to protect the appropriate religious expression of students, and that the relevant rules and standards would be communicated to the teaching faculty so that similar infringements and misunderstandings will not occur in the future.

"No student, no matter how old, should ever feel afraid to compassionately share his sincere religious beliefs with his classmates in appropriate times and manners," said June Jantz, attorney and former litigation coordinator at the Pacific Justice Institute in a press release. "We applaud the courage and testimony of this kindergarten student

14

and his mother in standing up for their right to read the boy's chosen religious book in class."

Standing By the Word of God

It is our responsibility to be bold for what is right according to the Word of God. What would you have done if you were in the school I just talked about? Would you be willing to take a stand for the sake of the young, innocent children who are bombarded by a pro-homosexual agenda? As a parent, would you be willing to stand up for your child's right to express his religious views? Many are timid about standing by the Word of God when it has the potential to create a ruckus. Reading through the Gospels reminds us that Christ was not afraid to make a ruckus in the name of truth. The New Testament, especially the book of Acts, focuses on the apostles' goal to take a stand for the Gospel, regardless of the circumstances. We are not alone in this challenge. Be reminded of the verse in Joshua, which says, *"Be strong and courageous. Do not be afraid or terrified; do not be discouraged, for the Lord your God will be with you, wherever you go."*[6]

15

2

TRUTH BE TOLD
Evangelizing Public Schools

*". . .all Americans are guaranteed the free exercise
of religion. Our children do not give up that
freedom when they enter the schoolroom door."*
Dr. James Dobson

While this book focuses on the legal basis for evangelizing in public schools, many philosophical arguments can also be made. For example, teachers teach students character decisions every day. While the main purpose of schooling is academic, in order to achieve success, discipline and order is essential. We cannot help that this discipline is derived from biblically based morals. For example, teachers and school administrators instruct their students not to steal and not to lie. While some people call these rules, others may call them a part of the Ten Commandments. Either way, these instructions are important for discipline and order so the student can achieve academically. Also, many schools have activities or lessons based on a variety of religious holidays that take place during the school year. Some consider this wrong, but others do not, based on the fact that these holidays are widely celebrated as a part of American culture and history.

Probably the greatest argument to be made for teaching students about Christianity is the fact that we live in a nation that was founded on biblical principles. If there is any doubt in your mind about that, I encourage you to study our nation's history, our historical documents, and many of the great men who fought for our nation with a primary purpose of freedom of religion. As Dr. James Dobson reminds us in his book *Children At Risk*,

*"Engraved on the cap on the top of the Washington
Monument are the words: 'Praise be to God.' As a*

17

tourist climbs the winding stairs inside they see such phrases as 'Search the Scriptures,' and 'Holiness to the Lord.'

At the Lincoln memorial the President's words are chiseled into granite: '...That this nation, under God, shall have a new birth of freedom, and that government of the people, by the people, for the people shall not perish from the earth.' On the south bank of the Tidal Basin sits the magnificent Jefferson Memorial with Jefferson's words, 'Can the liberties of a nation be secure when we have removed a conviction that these liberties are the gift of God. Indeed I tremble for my country when I reflect that God is just, that His justice cannot sleep forever.'[7]

The degree to which all of the founding fathers were practicing Christians can be challenged; however, according to our own historical documents, we are a nation founded on Christian practices and on the Word of God. Therefore, in teaching the basic and accurate history of this great nation we are unintentionally teaching Christian principles. If we are teaching properly, we cannot help but do so. We also find God in science, mathematics, literature, and more. For example, in the public high school I attended, my English teacher, who likely was not a Christian, used the Bible as literature. The Bible has also found an audience, as literature, in Orange County, California. Offered as one of various electives, the Bible as literature is becoming increasingly popular.

The Big Lie—Separation of Church and State

Sometimes when I speak at conferences, universities, or churches, I mention something called "the big lie." "The big lie," I say, "is the separation of _____" Then I let the audience fill in the blank, and they always do, without fail. It's the big lie we have all heard over and over again, the "separation of church and state." It is also one reason given by people when they say that students and teachers have no right whatsoever to read their Bible or share their faith during school hours. Let's set the record straight. *Nowhere in the Constitution does it mention the phrase, "separation of church and state."*

18

The "separation of church and state" actually comes from a letter written by Thomas Jefferson where *he expressed his concern over government meddling in the affairs of churches*, not the other way around. In fact the present majority in the Supreme Court have made it clear that government is not to be hostile to religion and should engage in benign neutrality.[8] *So the next time a school administrator, teacher, or government official attempts to silence you with the* big lie, *just ask him or her to show you where it is in the Constitution.*

For further study on the original intent of the Constitution concerning the issue of "separation of church and state" see *Wallbuilders Ministry* (see website list in back of book). Recommended reading regarding this topic: *Real Threat and Mere Shadow* by Daniel L. Dreisbach.

What Does the Law Say?

We can use several philosophical arguments for sharing faith in the public schools. In the end, however, you will want to know what the law says and what you are up against before you jump into this challenge. (see App. 2, 3, 4 and 5) At this point, some thoughts may be running through your mind, "Why know what the law is? If God wants me to share my faith with a student, teacher, or parent, shouldn't I do so regardless of the law? After all, we are talking about eternal life here. It is for only a short while that we are on this earth. In fact, this world is not even our home. We are aliens and strangers here and our ultimate goal should be to share Christ at all costs." As a Christian, these may be the thoughts going through your mind right now. In fact, you may be wondering if we are not, in fact, compromising the message of evangelism by exhorting you to know what the law is before you evangelize.

The fact is God wants us all to be wise and discerning when it comes to our opportunities to evangelize. Our earlier observation of the apostle Paul lays a clear foundation for why that is so important. He was aware of what the law said, and took advantage of it for the Kingdom.

But aren't there great disputes about what the law and Constitution say regarding religious freedom at public schools? While some disputes still exist, you may be surprised to learn there is universal agreement from both the left and the right regarding most issues of public school evangelism! See Appendix 3 in the back of this book to find a statement of agreement made by those usually on opposite sides of issues.[9] *In fact, by far the greatest curtailment of evangelism in public schools is not the absence of legal opportunities, but the ignorance of legal opportunities.*

What if I break the law but am convinced that God is calling me to share?

We want to make our position on this very clear. God may be clearly calling you to share your faith with a student, teacher, administrator, or parent in a way that defies the law. You must, however, be prepared to face the potential consequences, including possibly losing your job.

It may surprise you to know the lengths the law gives a person to share his or her faith. **Christians are not as restricted to share their faith as most people assume.** (see App. 2, 3, 4 and 5) The purpose of this book is to open your eyes to see all that you can do to evangelize and still abide by the law. The day may come when the law forbids us from sharing. When that day comes, as Scripture says, we are to share anyway. In Acts 4:18-19 we can read how Peter and John, before the Sanhedrin, respond to the order that they are not to preach the Gospel.

> *"Then they called them in again and commanded them not to speak or teach at all in the name of Jesus. But Peter and John replied, 'Judge for yourselves whether it is right in God's sight to obey you rather than God. For we cannot help speaking about what we have seen and heard.'"*

Once again, we do not share our faith because we are on the side of the law, but because we are on the side of the Lord.

3

I DARE YOU TO ASK ME ABOUT JESUS
Student-Initiated Evangelism

*"One word of truth shall outweigh
the whole world."*
Aleksandr Solzhenitsyn

Susanne shares a lot of youth ministry stories with me. One story she shared caused me to think about the boldness of students to evangelize. Here is the story from her point of view.

I remember the first time my co-worker in ministry and I saw a radical new t-shirt design. It was a t-shirt designed by a friend, Keith Poletiek, and it was meant to shake things up a bit. It did! On the back was written, in large, very readable letters, *"I Dare You To Ask Me About Jesus."* Then it had a silhouette of Jesus in the background. It was at a time when t-shirts were really taking off, especially with youth groups. Our friend Keith was quite the dominant force in the shirt business because he was creative and affordable. (Both of these items are very important for a youth minister to consider.) Keith's goal was to get as many students as possible wearing this shirt for the purpose of evangelism at their schools. We liked the idea and most of our youth did, too. Some were a bit intimidated, but we just encouraged them to be honest and transparent and share how Jesus had transformed their life. Without question, wearing this shirt made an impact in their lives because they had to be ready and willing to answer questions and share about Christ in their lives.

How Far Should We Go?

Susanne's story reminds me of how bold students can be when witnessing about Christ. What students often do not know is how far they ought to go in sharing, especially according to the law.

One day a junior high student named Matt asked a friend if he would like to visit Matt's church youth group and learn about Jesus. The friend said he was not interested. The next day Matt approached him again and asked him the same question. The friend said again that he was not interested. The following day Matt again repeated his question, then held up a piece of burnt toast in the student's face asking him if he wanted to look like that piece of burnt toast. That student eventually went to the principal's office and asked to have his schedule changed so he would not have to see Matt anymore.

The above story is not true, but it is one I like to tell when speaking to groups about evangelizing in their schools. It is an example of what could be considered harassment and should not be done at school, or anywhere for that matter. Students in all grades are allowed to share about their faith in a variety of ways. However, they should not repeatedly push people to listen to them when the other students have made it clear they are not interested. Not only does this border on harassment and could possibly get them in trouble, but practically speaking, it's not the best way to lovingly and convincingly evangelize. In contrast, the mere sharing of one's faith is not harassment simply because the peer hearing the message somehow finds it "offensive." We need to recognize that God has respected everyone's right to accept or reject Him. Christians should do no less as they boldly, yet lovingly, share their faith with others.

What If I Share My Faith and Get Into Trouble?

If students encounter problems with a teacher, administrator, parent, or fellow student, they have a couple of options. First of all, students should not get angry and yell about their rights. Of course, they do have rights so they therefore should not throw up their hands in surrender and give up sharing their faith. Rather, they ought to calmly and clearly explain that, according to the law, they have every right to share their faith. (see App. 3, 5) If the student stays within the limits of the law, he/she should have no problems. A student who has abided by

22

the law and still encounters problems should contact the Pacific Justice Institute. The following describes some examples of the areas in which Pacific Justice Institute has pledged to defend a student's right to share his/her faith with others.

Revival Rallies on Campus

One day a parent called to complain about a special assembly that was put on at her son's high school. The assembly consisted of two guest speakers with a pro-homosexuality presentation. After examining the facts, along with the legal options, an attorney challenged this parent to be proactive. Although there was nothing that could be done because the assembly had already taken place in accordance with the existing law, the parent could work with his or her student to present an opposing view to homosexuality at his school.

> *"The first step," the attorney explained, "is for your son to start a Bible club at his school." (The key to starting a Bible club can be found in the next section. Also see Appendix 3, 5.)*
>
> *"What if they don't let him?" the mother responded a bit tentatively.*
>
> *"If he has any roadblocks from the principal, just give me a call," replied the attorney. "Most schools will cooperate. Next, the Bible club should arrange to reserve use of the school gym, or other room, when it is not being used by another club or school activity. The club can invite an outside speaker and a band. They can also pass out flyers and put up posters to announce the event."*
>
> *The surprised mother hesitantly responded, "Are you sure this is okay in a public school?"*

We have found that most parents, teachers, students, school admin-istrators and youth ministers are not fully aware of their or their students' rights regarding religion in public schools. The attorney informed this mother of her son's rights according to already existing law. If the school allows other non-curriculum related clubs to have meetings, put up posters, and invite outside speakers, then, generally, the school must allow the same for religious clubs.

23

The mother took to heart these instructions . . . and so did her son. A few months later, she called to give us some great news. The parent informed us that her son had, in fact, started a Bible club on his school campus. Not only did he start a Bible club, he also organized a revival rally on campus. Approximately two hundred high school students attended, and several made decisions to receive Christ as their Lord and Savior! *It was exciting to hear from a parent and student who took to heart their rights as citizens with the ultimate goal of spreading the good news of Christ.*

The idea of having revival rallies at public schools is very close to our hearts for a few reasons. First of all, there are so many youth getting the wrong message about relationships, sexuality, drugs, and other moral issues. This is a perfect opportunity to send the right message to youth who are searching for morality and meaning to life. Second, schools generally cannot stop it. In a bold and heartening decision for those who value both church and state, the United States Supreme Court made it very clear that if schools allow other groups on campus after school to use their facilities, they have to allow churches and Christian clubs to utilize it as well.[10] Consequently, a church could sponsor a rally at virtually any high school, junior high, or even an elementary school, so long as other outside groups have been allowed to access the facilities as well. This court ruling becomes particularly powerful in states like California that actually *require* public schools to grant access to school facilities to certain outside groups (e.g., the Boy Scouts).

Also, organizing revival rallies on public school campuses will no doubt multiply youth ministries. Whether you are a student, youth minister, or parent reading this book, we strongly encourage you to consider this exciting opportunity. It is an opportunity to bring in worship bands, dynamic speakers, and testimonies from people who previously dealt with drug addiction, promiscuity, or homosexuality before they found the Lord. Does this sound overwhelming to you? Well, you do not have to do it on your own! Talk to others in your church. Talk to your pastor. Help them see a vision of young people gathering after school, *in their school*, to hear the Gospel creatively presented through music, testimonies and speakers! If you are a youth pastor, network with area youth pastors and collectively organize a revival rally at a local school. (And if you need any practical or legal guidance, just remember that Pacific Justice Institute is here to help you too!)

The Key to Legally Starting a Student-Led Bible Club: The Equal Access Act

Now for some lawyer talk (Don't worry – it is easy to understand!) Where do these opportunities to start Bible clubs come from? For high school students, the answer lies in the Equal Access Act.[11] (You can find the Equal Access Act in Appendix 2 in the back of this book.) This legislation, in a nutshell, states that a public secondary school (usually grades nine through twelve) must not exclude or discriminate against religious or political clubs as long as students comply with the following conditions:

1) The club must be both created and run by the students. The school usually requires a teacher to volunteer as a sponsor. The teacher attends the Bible club but does not participate in any way.

2) The club must meet during non-instructional time. This requirement basically refers to lunch time or after school.

3) The school has other non-curriculum related clubs. If the school you are attending has other non-curriculum related clubs, you can begin a Bible club which has the same benefits as existing on-campus clubs.

4) The school receives some federal funding. In other words, if you attend a public school, the Equal Access Act will likely apply.

Bible Club Not Allowed To Mention Bible in Their Advertising

A California high school Bible club in the Lodi Unified School District was faced with opposition. The club was told they could not use the word "Bible" in their announcements over the PA system, because the word "Bible" may "be offensive" to some of the students. A concerned parent whose child attends the high school and was informed of this restriction contacted the Pacific Justice Institute. After intervention by one of our attorneys, the school is now allowing the club the same rights to the PA system announcements as the other clubs.

Occasionally, a high school will try to contend that it has no non-curriculum related clubs and therefore should be allowed to prohibit religious clubs. Few, if any high schools will be able to pass this scrutiny. One federal district court has already held that pep rally clubs constitute a non-curriculum club.[12] Few high schools will sacrifice pep rallies in order to keep out religion.

There will be those, however, who will do practically anything to keep Bible clubs off campus.[13] A recent Pacific Justice Institute case, which has become very newsworthy, is the Saddleback school case. In this particular case, FCA (Fellowship of Christian Athletes) was told they could not meet on school grounds during the lunch period. After litigation, the state appellate court ruled 3-0 that the school district had to allow the Bible club on campus since it already allowed on campus other non-curriculum related clubs. (See App. 3) However, shortly after the ruling, the school district canceled all non-curriculum clubs.

In fact, one of their senior staff was quoted as blaming the Bible club for the new policy. While preparing for continued litigation for this clearly discriminatory and hostile action, we received word that the school board actually decided to reverse its position. Even though the decision to make this change took several months, we are pleased that the school board realizes that schools cannot be discriminatory on the basis of religious beliefs. We hope others will follow suit!

The Equal Access Act is a strong defense for the existence of Bible clubs, and thousands of high schools in the United States have respected the rights of students to start these clubs. In addition, the club is free to invite outside speakers including pastors, youth pastors, and directors of ministries. However, the students should be careful not to have the same speaker appear so often that there is the appearance that someone is leading the club other than the students. In her career as a youth minister, my wife Susanne had the opportunity to help students begin clubs and she also spoke before a number of these clubs. Here is one experience she tells which took place on a high school campus.

At one school in Rowland Heights, California, my co-worker and I were kicked off the high school campus for being there "too often." Unfortunately, "too often" to the principal meant more than once a year. This happened a number of years ago and at that time my co-worker and I made a few calls to the school and spoke with the science teacher (an elder at our church) to see what he could do for us. Finally, after frustrating attempts, we decided to lay low for awhile. Had this happened a few years later, we could have called the Pacific Justice Institute to ask for advice. Eventually, we got back onto the campus although we were hardly welcomed with open arms.

Sometimes schools will attempt to prevent religious clubs from meeting during lunch time claiming that "non-instructional" time is only before and after school. (See App. 3) This was exactly the issue in the *Ceniceros v. San Diego* U.S.D. case where the 9th Circuit Court of Appeals held that "non-instructional" time includes lunch time, entitling religious clubs in California to meet during lunch.[14]

"Easter" Food Drive Canned

In March of 2002, an annual canned food drive was underway at a high school in Hampton, Virginia. The Christian club on campus, "Warriors for Christ" collected non-perishable food for the needy for the annual Easter Can Drive it sponsors for a local YMCA Women's Shelter. However, this year the club was informed by their faculty advisor that the name would have to be changed from "Easter Can Drive" to "Spring Can Drive." A fellow student, not a member of the Warriors for Christ club, alerted the Pacific Justice Institute to this situation. The student also started a petition on behalf of the club and had the support of many other students to maintain the Easter name. The club was advised that the reason for the required change was due to how the name "Easter" might be offensive to students of other religions. The Pacific Justice Institute represented the club. For reasons unknown to us at this time, the students capitulated and changed the name.

Not Just a Bible Club

As evidenced by the Easter food drive story, a Bible club does not have to simply be a group of Christians meeting on the public school campus to read the Bible. There are tremendous opportunities for Bible clubs including the aforementioned revival rally, community service projects and participation in outside crusades and events. While it is a great encouragement for Christian students to meet, pray and study the Bible, many opportunities for ministry present themselves in the public school. For example, use this club as an opportunity to organize a community service project. Better yet, organize a service project which benefits the school itself. Other opportunities include passing out invitations to the Harvest Crusade or a Billy Graham Crusade, or organizing a National Day of Prayer event. Just remember, the opportunities are endless to make a positive impact on your school campus through the Bible or Christian club.

What If I Am Faced With Opposition?

While the easiest response for a student faced with opposition is to merely accept what the administrator or teacher says at face value without checking into it, calling an organization like the Pacific Justice Institute for help can often solve the problem. We can inform you if you are within your rights, and we can assist you as needed. Another student in Southern California did not just sit back and do nothing. After the Christian club on his campus was told that they could not meet in the quad and use the sound system, even though every other club could, (see App. 3) this student called the Pacific Justice Institute to find out what the law said on this issue. The attorney spoke with the superintendent of this school district. The attorney explained the situation, found there to be a misunderstanding, and the superintendent assured that attorney that there would be no more problems in the future. *It is always refreshing and encouraging seeing a student stand up for his or her rights with an attitude that still honors the name of Christ.* While you may face some opposition, knowing what the law says about your rights as a student is important when organizing a Bible club. Don't forget that the apostle Paul also faced opposition when sharing the Gospel. Paul did not cower, nor did he get angry. Rather, he stated his rights clearly and in a loving manner that glorified God. Simply follow Paul's example in order to effectively impact your school for Christ.

What about Junior Highs or Elementary Schools?

A question we are often asked is, "Are Bible clubs under protection on junior high campuses also?" While it is true that junior high schools do not generally fall under the protection of the Equal Access Act, the federal 8th Circuit Court of Appeals has held that the U.S. Constitution's First Amendment guarantees protection to religious gatherings in both junior high and elementary schools.[15] In the end, you should be successful if you want to begin a Bible club on your child's campus.

I'm Just a Student – What Can I Do?

Stephanie* was an eighth grade student in Southern California. She made up her mind that her school needed a Bible club, and that she was the one to start it. She spoke with her youth pastor and then

*Name has been change to protect privacy

28

arranged a meeting between him and her principal to discuss the possibility of organizing such a club. The meeting went well, and she was an active participant in organizing the club's activities and speakers. Stephanie took action and made a difference in the lives of many.

Amy* was a junior in high school, and she wanted to make a difference for the Lord and in the lives of her friends. She attended a church where the average attendance was around five to six hundred. A church of that size would generally have a youth group averaging approximately fifty students. Amy was not content to stop at the average. Every Wednesday morning before school, she would meet her youth pastor at 6:30 a.m. in the youth building at the church. They would pray for that evening's youth service, then pray over each chair and for the specific student who would be sitting in it that evening. Her concern for her fellow students did not end there. She then went on to school where she would invite a number of people, both friends and acquaintances to youth group. Others followed her example and also invited their friends to youth group. Because Amy was not content to simply sit back and watch the world pass her by, God blessed not only her prayers, but her inviting as well. God blessed that youth group and it grew to an average of one hundred and twenty, with many accepting the Lord and being baptized. Amy was just a student, yet she made a difference where it mattered most.

"I'm just a student, what can I do?" This question may actually be your excuse for not taking action for the Lord. As can be observed by the previous examples and more to come, a student can take much action and be an active participant in evangelism, especially at school. We hope that these examples of pro-active students will encourage you and motivate you to take action and make a difference in the lives of many. Read on to discover the many legal ways you can evangelize at your public school.

ONE ON ONE EVANGELISM

Christian clubs are great and contribute to the spreading of the gospel and the encouragement of Christian students on campus. It is important to remember, however, that evangelism and spiritual growth are usually best done on a relational level. Many have come to know the Lord in a group setting; however, in order to understand and grow in the Lord, that same person needs to develop relationships, one on

*Name has been change to protect privacy

one, with another individual. Also, some people respond better when the Gospel is shared with them in a one-on-one conversation. That way they feel comfortable asking questions about what it means to be a Christian. Irrespective of whether or not the school has a religious club, students and individuals have tremendous opportunities to share their faith. While students do have every right to share their faith with others, they ought to remember the rights of anyone not interested in listening. As stated previously, if a student is continually sharing with another student who does not want to listen, that first student needs to find someone else to share with. Also remember, nothing prevents students from praying for any other student.

TALENT SHOWS AND LIP SYNCS

One day our office received the following phone call: "Hello, my nine-year-old daughter was going to sing a Christian song for the school talent show, but was told she couldn't because it was religious. Is that legal?"

The attorney asked if the students were allowed to choose their own song to sing. The parent said they were, as long as the song was not religious. The attorney then sent a letter to the principal explaining that the school cannot engage in discrimination against the songs chosen by students simply because of the song's religious content. (See App. 3)

Though some alleged legal rights organizations seem to vacillate on this legal issue, the Pacific Justice Institute works hard to defend student-initiated religious speech. This school, like many, overreacted in order to ensure that the ACLU (American Civil Liberties Union) would not sue them. However, once the school understood what the law said regarding this particular issue, it quickly reversed its position and allowed the student to sing the religious song.

If given the opportunity, choosing to use a talent show or lip sync to spread the Gospel is a great plan! Creative young people can use Christian music and ideas for their school's talent shows and lip syncs. The college Susanne attended held an annual lip sync (where the students perform and mouth the words to a song that is being played) and the students had a lot of fun choosing their favorite songs to perform. Be bold, be brave, and be creative for the sake of the Gospel and for the sake of your fellow students.

In Morgan Hill, California, two girls named Brigitte and Joanna* were told they could not dance to "We Can Make A Difference," a song by Jaci Velasque* for their school's talent show. They were told that because of the song's religious nature, they could not use it. (See App. 3) Their mother immediately contacted Pacific Justice Institute for assistance. A PJI attorney then contacted the school district on behalf of the family. The school district responded by quickly acknowledging the mistake, and granted the girls permission to perform to their selection. The bottom line is that a student's song or skit selection for a talent show or lip sync must not be prohibited because of its religious content when the selection is the student's choice and not the result of teacher initiation.

BOOK REPORTS

Teachers will often allow students to choose what book they would like to read and then assign the student to do an oral or written book report. Book reports, especially ones that are done orally, provide a tremendous opportunity for evangelism. As long as the book chosen is age appropriate, not obscene, and falls within the assigned subject matter, the teacher cannot forbid a book report on a chosen book simply because of its religious content.[16]

For example, if a teacher assigns the students to read a book about a hero, a student should feel free to choose books about religious heroes such as A.C. Green, Corrie Ten Boom, Chuck Colson, or even Jesus Christ.[17] Josh* attends a public high school in Auburn, California. When assigned a book report, he chose *Left Behind*, by Jerry Jenkins and Tim LaHaye. This Christian fictional book contained a lot of scripture and talked about the end times. He had no problems with his teacher and was able to use this book as a witnessing tool. The bottom line is, if a student is assigned to write a book report on a favorite book, the student should feel free to use a biblically based book or an autobiography of a Christian.

We have heard of occasions where a teacher will allow the student to read a book that contains religious content, but then will prevent the student from sharing it orally before the class as all the other students had done. (See App. 3) Pacific Justice Institute would argue that such an action is unconstitutional and that the public school is acting hostile to religion; therefore, it is violating the First Amendment's Establish-

*Name has been changed to protect privacy.

ment and Free Speech Clauses. (See App. 3) In addition, if the teacher is completely open-ended about what book a student may choose, a student could possibly do a report on a book of the Bible or other religious text as long as it meets the teacher's length requirements. As you can see, many legal (and we emphasize, legal) opportunities are available to share your faith, even in the classroom.

ART OR CRAFT PROJECTS

In elementary schools, students are often given holiday projects to make. It is ironic to hear about holiday (literally "holy day") projects, yet in the same breath hear about the "separation of church and state". As stated previously, teachers ought to know that this "separation of church and state" phrase is never uttered in the Constitution. These school projects may include Valentines to be given to other classmates or Mother's and Father's Day cards to be taken home. The school generally cannot reject how the student constructs a card or project simply because it conveys a religious message with elements such as a cross or a Bible verse. (See App. 3) Such hostility to religion would likely be held unconstitutional.

SHARING WITH TEACHERS

Of course, the first step in reaching out to teachers is by working hard and behaving well. With that said, students need to realize they have the liberty to share their faith with their teacher, both directly and indirectly. When the student writes a paper expressing his or her faith, the teacher *has to read it.* But students can also be creative. Some students may (with parental consent) invite their teacher over for dinner. Students may also give their teachers holiday cards with a distinct religious message. Gateways to Better Education (See website list in back of book.) offers unique cards with a meaning, including a brief summary of what the law says regarding religious expression in public schools.

RELIGIOUS CLOTHING

Do you remember the T-shirt mentioned at the beginning of this chapter: the *I Dare You to Ask Me about Jesus* shirt? It definitely generated lots of attention and questions. Under the pretext of not wanting to "offend" other students, schools in the past have attempted to prohibit students from wearing T-shirts with a religious message. In one circumstance, the school insisted the student turn the shirt inside out or face suspension. What was the "offensive" message in *Real Men Follow Jesus?* The school administrators quickly reversed their policy once they were informed of the unconstitutionality of their action. (See App. 3) The fact is schools generally cannot forbid clothing or buttons from being worn by students simply because of their religious content. The obvious exception would be schools that require school uniforms. Also, at least one court has ruled that "religious" speech on T-shirts is not protected if it also can be construed as hate speech.[18] Otherwise, you should generally have no problem wearing clothing with a religious message.

GRADUATION SPEECHES

A few years ago, the Supreme Court ruled that school-initiated graduation prayers are unconstitutional.[19] This controversial ruling resulted in many school districts attempting to censor valedictorians or their pre-qualified graduation speakers from having *any* religious content in their speeches.

Pacific Justice Institute has counseled and represented a number of individuals regarding this matter. We were contacted by a group of high school students in Northern California who were concerned about the proposed policy for graduation speeches. This school district presented a mixed message to its students, parents, and teachers. The written policy stated that religious content would be subject to disapproval by the school administrators. What made this policy even more interesting was when the school board members, during their meeting, actually stated verbally that it was acceptable for students to talk about God or Jesus during their speech. This was in direct contradiction to written policy. One of our attorneys tried to point out the obvious contradiction to the school board. "If the school board was comfortable with a student speaker using religious speech, why couldn't that be stated in their written policy?" the attorney reasoned with the board. The board was fearful of being sued by an opposing entity to that policy change; however, the thought of being sued by a pro-religious freedom group had not even occurred to them. By the end of the meeting, the school board voted to wait and study the issue further before approval of the proposed written policy.

33

In situations such as this, it is important to remember the distinction between student-initiated and state-initiated religious speech. The prior is protected while the latter is not. Consequently, the school must not attempt to censor a student's speech simply on the basis of its religious content. (See App. 3) Instead, if the school has concerns over the semblance of school endorsement of the student's religious viewpoint, it should simply recite or include a disclaimer in the program. For example, the disclaimer could say, "The content of the student's speech is that of the student, and not necessarily that of the school district or its employees."

At least one Federal Circuit Court allowed a school district to censor a valedictorian's religious speech.[20] However, other circuit courts have found that as long as the district policy is neutral, religious content can be presented during a graduation speech.[21] The United States Supreme Court chose to let this decision stand, thereby allowing student-led religious speech during graduation.[22] As a result of these conflicting decisions, the Supreme Court will have to definitively rule on this issue in the future.

In addition, some courts have upheld the constitutionality of having an official invocation as long as the students vote beforehand to have the prayer, a student is chosen by the students to deliver the prayer, and the school has no input in the prayer's content.[23] However, in view of the recent ruling in *Santa Fe Independent School District v. Jane Doe*[24], such voting practices to specifically elect a religious speaker are less likely to withstand court scrutiny. The court ruling, however, does not go so far as to approve of the censoring of a student speaker because of his or her religious viewpoint (e.g. recite Scripture or pray) when the speaker was chosen to speak based upon secular criteria (i.e. student was the valedictorian).[25] In the policy section of this book you will find a model policy regarding graduation speeches that can be recommended to school boards and/or administrators.

PASSING OUT TRACTS, FLYERS, ETC.

Youth pastors can sometimes become discouraged because of their difficulty in inviting students to church-related events. While pastors may have some difficulties passing out flyers during school hours, the students themselves are generally free to pass out such announcements.[26] Youth pastors simply need to give flyers and tracts to the members of their youth group so they can pass them out at school.

Okay, students! This is your chance to do something simple, yet effective in the way of evangelism. If *you* are reading this book, not your youth pastor, let your pastor know that if he or she made flyers about various events at your church, including a Bible study or lock-in, that you would be willing to pass them out! (This is also something children can do in their elementary schools.) Just be sure not to pass them out in a way that disrupts your class (like during a test or during classroom instruction). You also have the freedom to pass out Christian tracts, Bibles, books or videos as long as it is not disruptive. (See App. 3) Take the opportunity of Bible clubs or revival rallies to get Bibles out into your school. Talk to your youth pastor who probably knows how to get hold of a large number of Bibles. Any youth pastor would love to have students asking for Bibles to pass out at their public school.

School Intolerant of Student Religious Speech

A second grader attending a public elementary school in Palm Desert, California, was prevented from passing out videos to his peers during a gift exchange. After learning that the gifts were a religious video about creation, the principal absolutely prohibited the second grader from passing out the videos. Upon being informed by the second grader's grandmother of the situation, the Pacific Justice Institute sent a legal demand letter to the school's principal and superintendent. The school district's attorney responded to the letter by alleging that "distribution of a religious videotape disrupts orderly operations of the classroom, invades the rights of others, and subjects the students to the potential for coercion and proselytizing of a particular religious doctrine." The school had initially advised the grandmother that students were not allowed to pass out gifts in the classroom even though other students had in fact exchanged gifts. However, later the second grader was allowed to pass out videos that the school deemed non-religious. The Pacific Justice Institute assisted the grandmother in filing an administrative complaint against the school district.

Students often pass up this evangelism opportunity because they do not think they will be allowed to pass out flyers about a youth event or give away tracts or videos like the student we just mentioned. Students are generally free to pass out such announcements and may also give their friends Gospel tracts, books, videos, etc. during recess, at lunch, or before and after class.

READING THE BIBLE AND PRAYING

Students in public schools should know that the school cannot forbid them from praying or reading their Bible or other religious books during non-curriculum (before school, recess, lunchtime, after school) time. Since students have an unequivocal right to distribute religious literature on campus, it is only logical that students would be able to then read religious literature on campus as well.[27] This principle does not just apply to students who pray or read alone, it also applies to instances where students decide to pray, read, or discuss religion together. (See App. 3) There is no law (none that would be found constitutional at least) that forbids students, alone or in a group, from praying, reading, and/or discussing religion during non-curriculum time at school.

Although courts have never directly addressed the issue of whether a student may read their Bible during curriculum time, in the proper circumstances it should be allowed. As long as the students do not disrupt the educational process or interfere with other students' rights to be let alone, then they should be allowed to read their Bible even during curriculum time at school.[28] Obviously a student could not start reading his or her Bible while the teacher was in the middle of a lesson, but the student should be allowed to read the Bible during silent reading time or any time when other students are allowed to read quietly.

Prayer Protest is Squashed by Basketball Team

In Sacramento, California, the Pacific Justice Institute committed to defend the rights of students at a local high school to pray at the state finals basketball game. This pledge came after Americans United for Separation of Church and State threatened the school district with a lawsuit which protested the students praying before their basketball games. The coach of the team was also attacked for his willingness to stand next to the students and bow his head during their prayer time. The students had a choice to make. Should they stand for their right to pray, or should they buckle under the threat of a lawsuit? The community wondered what would happen the night of the big game. Friday night came, and the crowd witnessed two events. First, Coach Troy Larson* prayed with several local pastors on the basketball court just

*Name has been changed to protect privacy

36

before the commencement of the state championship. And second, at the center of the basketball court, a group of basketball players also prayed before the game.

After the school district had received the letter from Americans United for Separation of Church and State (AUSCS) threatening litigation, and the coach had allegedly been told that neither he nor the students would be allowed to pray at all, Pacific Justice Institute intervened in the matter to ensure that the coach's free exercise rights would not be infringed. We committed to defend both the coach and the students should legal action be brought for their open prayer before the basketball game.

Although the 5th Circuit Court of Appeals has held that teacher/coach initiated prayer before games is an unconstitutional entanglement of the state and religion,[29] student initiated prayer should be allowed.[30] To be upheld as constitutional however, the prayer must be clearly student initiated and run, the prayer cannot be disruptive to others, and the prayer cannot be forced onto students who do not want to participate.[31]

In another case, the Duncanville Unified School District, near Dallas, Texas, was sued by the ACLU for allowing a group of basketball players to hold hands and pray while standing on the court before every basketball game.[29] Since the students, and not the coach, initiated the praying, the Fifth Circuit Court of Appeals upheld the District's allowance of the students to pray.

See You at the Pole

See You at the Pole is a prayer event that is familiar to many students, teachers, and parents. School districts cannot forbid students from praying around a flagpole when prayer is initiated by students and does not disrupt instruction (i.e. class time, assembly, etc.) It is even permissible for teachers to be present at these prayer meetings "in a passive or supervisory capacity," as long as they do not initiate the gathering.[32] Without question, students enrolled in public schools have many opportunities to evangelize. The students often only need to be aware of their rights and be encouraged to share their faith boldly.

37

It's Okay to Take a Stand for what is Right. . . Even in the Classroom

Dave Miller* had a decision to make. He was in his high school English class, and his teacher was discussing the book *Grapes of Wrath*. It sounds harmless enough, but the teacher was discussing all of the homosexual characters in the novel. If you have ever read this book, you know there are no homosexual characters in it. Dave finally got fed up and stood up to leave the class. The teacher said to him, "What's wrong, Dave? Are you not mature enough to handle this kind of discussion?"

"No," Dave said. "As soon as you start teaching English and stop pushing your social agenda, I'll be back." Then he walked out and went to the principal's office and called his parents. His parents came down to the school and filed a formal complaint. Dave did have to deal with some consequences for his actions. Usually, when you stand up for what is right, you *do* have to deal with consequences.

The next day the teacher told his English class that because Dave's parents filed a formal complaint, he might be fired. He "just wanted them all to know." This was a difficult time for Dave, but what the teacher may not have realized is that he had violated the law when he offered this incorrect information to his class. Dave's parents called the Pacific Justice Institute who came to his defense. The teacher was demoted, and the school promised this would never happen again. Why? Because one student stood up to what was wrong and stood up for what was right.

Run the Race, Stay on Course, Share Your Faith

The point of sharing Dave's story is not for you, as a student, to become a sort of vigilante, seeking out teachers to destroy. In fact, teachers need to know the Lord as much as your fellow students do, and we pray that Dave's teacher will come to know Christ. It is okay, though, to take a stand for what is right. We have had a number of students who have had to deal with similar situations to Dave's. These students chose to go home, share with their parents what happened, and work with them to decide the best course of action. We often receive calls from parents asking for help, and we contact the school in an attempt to get matters resolved in the least offensive way pos-

*Name has been changed to protect privacy.

sible. Why? It is the Paul principle we shared in an earlier chapter. If you remember, Paul looked at everyone from centurions to those in Caesar's household as potential followers of God. In the same way, every administrator, teacher, and student should also be viewed as a potential follower of God. Just as Paul stood up for what is right with the goal of seeing people won to the Lord, Christians should want to do the same. *Your ultimate goal as you run the race as a Christian is to stay on course and share your faith and God's love through the many opportunities God gives you!*

4

THE HIGH CALLING OF A TEACHER
Teacher-Initiated Evangelism

"It is impossible to rightly govern the world without God and the Bible." —George Washington

I am pleased and surprised at how many of our friends have become teachers. Most of them are elementary teachers and work in the public school system. We also know administrators and superintendents of some of the largest school districts in California. They are all good people, committed Christians, and dedicated to doing what is right and what is best for their students. This section of the book is focused on what teachers can do to evangelize in their schools. Because public schools have such enormous problems (that the Christian community often talks about), public school teachers who are Christians may feel demeaned or insecure about their chosen occupation. However, the goal of this book is not to do that. If you are in the public school system as a teacher, administrator, or staff member, you are in the trenches. And you are in the trenches willingly, desiring to make a difference for many young people who may be discouraged, on the verge of despair, or uncertain about their potential. You are to be commended for your hard work and dedication to students. However, you may also be put on the line at some point for your commitment to your faith.

Homosexual Theater Group Invades Elementary School

Take elementary teacher Mark Jones*, for example. He is a teacher in a fairly conservative part of the country, Orange County, California. He called Pacific Justice Institute in great distress because of an assembly that had just taken place. The activist homosexual group (mentioned earlier in the book) put on the assembly. This pro-homosexual

*Name has been changed to protect privacy

41

group performs skits and discusses how homosexuality is normal and natural.

(By the way, we heard of one little girl who came home after attending one of these assemblies at her school and told her mom she was a lesbian because she liked girls more than boys. Is there a problem? I definitely think so!)

Mr. Jones was immediately disturbed by the tone of the assembly and prepared his students to leave. The principal told Mr. Jones if he removed his class, he would be fired. Consequently, he let his class stay, but he was deeply disturbed and called Pacific Justice Institute to see if there was any recourse. There was little that could be done, explained one of our attorneys, because the assembly was already over, and no parents who may have known
of the assembly contacted us for help. This scenario is merely one example of what public school teachers have to deal with. The teacher, staff person, or administrator, will most likely encounter a time when a difficult decision has to be made. Following your convictions and obeying the Lord is important above all else, regardless of the consequences. However, it is still possible in most circumstances to comply with the school district's policies, while not compromising your convictions as a Christian.

Opportunities for Teachers

Without a doubt, teachers do not have the same degree of evangelism opportunities as students. The courts generally view teachers as government representatives. Therefore, this representation is the primary determination if what they do is too religious to be constitutional.[33] In other words, teachers do not have the same degree of freedom to share their faith that students do because they are actual representatives of the state, and the state, according to the courts, is not to promote one religion over another. While a teacher's opportunities are limited, she/he can still be influential in the lives of students, especially by being a good example and a positive influence.

However, keep in mind that a very practical element lies in whether the teacher has tenure, or is an "at will" employee. If the teacher has tenure, it is generally very difficult for the school district to terminate employment. If the teacher is an "at will" employee, he/she may be terminated without any explanation given. For this reason, teachers in some potentially hostile school districts might want to hold off on implementing some of the following suggestions until they receive tenure (i.e., usually in one to three years of service). While we want everyone to act on his or her conscience and on the Holy Spirit's prompting, waiting for tenure is simply a cautionary recommendation. With that said, let's discover the many exciting opportunities for evangelism of which teachers can take advantage!

Start with your Peers!

Title VII of the Civil Rights Act of 1964, *supra*, gives special protection for employees who feel compelled by their faith to engage in religious practices while at work (so long as it does not result in an undue hardship upon the employer). To cut to the chase, you as a teacher may generally use available space at the school and non-classroom time to conduct a Bible study on school grounds for fellow teachers. (Please notice that we said teachers and not students!) God has placed you in this particular school at this time for a reason. This is part of your *sphere of influence* or *oikos* that is mentioned in chapter eight in the section entitled, *Lifestyle Evangelism*. Take the opportunity to get to know your fellow teachers, staff, and administration. It is perfectly legal for you to pray for your peers and develop valuable friendships. If God is calling you to begin a Bible study or prayer time for your adult peers before or after school hours, you can do so. In fact, organizations like Fellowship and Christian Encouragement (FACE) for educators (www.prayingeducator.org) assist teachers in accomplishing such goals.

Classroom vs. Contract Time

Courts have made a distinction between a teacher's classroom time, when they are actually teaching the children and *contract* time, which is when a child approaches the teacher before or after class.[34] Consequently, in responding to a student's inquiry about the teacher's faith, the teacher might choose to identify his or her religion, but reserve any explanation of that faith only to the extent asked and only if asked to do so during contract time (i.e. non-classroom time). In fact, a federal court on appeal upheld a school district's policy forbidding a teacher from attempting to "convert students to Christianity or initiating conversations about your religious beliefs."[35]

Here is an illustration to ensure that this concept is understood. Say you are teaching your class a lesson about history. Religion is often a part of history instruction; therefore, it often is included in part of your discussion. If Johnny raises his hand and asks what religion you are, can you tell him? Yes. If a student asks about your faith or religion during classroom time, you can tell the class your religion without going into the theological points and citing Scripture. Your answer ought to be clear and concise without elaboration. If Johnny, or another student, raises his hand and asks you to elaborate, you can tell the student that the class needs to stay on track with the lesson; however, you would be glad to answer all such questions after class is over. The additional questions may then be answered, but only to the extent they are asked and in a non-converting manner! That way you are not subjecting your whole class of students to your beliefs, but you are not refusing to answer the academic questions of any interested student.

Curriculum Options

I attended a public high school in Texas, where my English teacher used a part of the Bible for her curriculum. She was teaching on poetry and used Psalms, among other books, as an example of poetry. Was she violating the law by promoting a religion? No, she was in no violation of the law. First of all, my teacher was likely not a Christian, and someone whose religious beliefs were speculative at best. She did, however, see the poetry of the Bible as a constructive teaching tool. Therefore, she definitely could not be accused of promoting her faith. Secondly, nothing prohibits a teacher from using the Bible in an educational, non-proselytizing manner. For example, the Bible has found an audience as literature, in Orange County, California. Offered as one of various electives, the Bible as literature is becoming increasingly popular. An organization called the National Council on Bible Curriculum in Public Schools has reportedly been successful at getting the Bible into as many as 183 school districts in 33 states. (See Website list, App. 6, in the back of the book.)

The most common legal issue that arises for teachers is often involving their choice of curriculum. One example that came to our attention was regarding a teacher who was going to be reprimanded for including creation along with evolution, in his class. This balanced approach is not unconstitutional. It is perfectly legal for a teacher to include all theories of the existence of man in his or her classroom. He or she cannot, however, demean one over another so as to show partiality because of his or her religious perspective.

In addition, teachers who are conscientiously opposed to giving certain types of instruction because of their beliefs can be accomodated.[36] If you refuse to teach evolution because of your Christian faith, you can request to be excused from that section, the school can bring in a substitute, and the kids will be taught their curriculum anyway. It just won't be you teaching it. However, at least one court did not allow a teacher to refuse to teach evolution.[37]

The best strategy for teachers is to teach both evolution and creation. How is that possible, you might ask? If you are asked to teach evolution, teach **all** of evolution – the evidence supporting–and opposing it. It is such a ridiculous theory to many, that the evidence will most likely speak for itself. Not only that, but in teaching this entire subject, you inherently include the theories debunking the theory of evolution, including spontaneous appearance or intelligent design. (However, one court determined that a school district's use of terms like "creation science" may be deemed to be "religious" and therefore found to be unconstitutional).[38] This is a proactive way of dealing with this type of opposition to your faith. If taught correctly, the validity of both will speak for itself.

We are also seeing more high school courses that include world religions and the history of religions, including Christianity. These courses are an excellent way to open students' minds to the truth that there is more to this life than just living and dying. You may also be able to bring in guest speakers from various religions. However, if you bring in a speaker from just one religion, a court could determine such a move to be an unconstitutional endorsement of one particular faith.

Classroom Projects & Traditional Holidays

An important part of classroom instruction, especially in elementary school, is learning by doing classroom projects and the acknowledgment of traditional, historical holidays. A teacher can instruct her class to design a collage, for example, with pictures displaying honesty and courage. If a student turns in a project with biblical or Christian figures or quotes, it is okay for the teacher to accept such a project. The teacher does not have to deny a project based on the inclusion of something religious. (See App. 3)

45

With regard to songs, teachers may choose religious songs to be sung by students as long as it does not appear that the teacher is proselytizing or endorsing religion.[39] For example, Christmas carols are as much a part of tradition as they are religion. Ask any person off the street and they could sing a Christmas carol to you, regardless of his or her religious or non-religious background. If you as the teacher choose Christmas carols to be sung, you might want to also include some songs recognizing the Hanukkah holiday as well in order to avoid the appearance of endorsing a particular faith. Similarly, teachers should not feel inhibited to temporarily display religious decorations (e.g. Nativity display) recognizing religious holidays for an instructional purpose.[40]

Elementary School Says Away with "Away in a Manger"

In San Diego, California, the San Diego Unified School District informed one of its teachers that she could not lead the children in singing the traditional Christmas carol, "Away in a Manger." The administration referenced the school district's policy, which forbade songs that would "be more appropriate in a house of worship or religious school". The teacher called the Pacific Justice Institute for representation. After one of our attorneys contacted the legal counsel for the school district, the administration reversed their position within twenty-four hours and allowed "Away in a Manger" to be sung. "Students need to know that our culture is based on full truth and historical fact, including the origin of holidays," said the teacher.

The Pacific Justice Institute is committed to defending the rights of teachers who have done nothing wrong in regard to school projects or religious instruction. The key is for all classroom projects, holiday acknowledgements, and religious instruction, to be carried out in an objective, non-proselytizing manner.

Teachers as Citizens

Although teachers are clearly limited in what they can do or say during work hours, teachers are generally entitled to the same rights as other citizens or outside organizations to interact with students in religious settings, on or off school grounds after school hours.[41] Teacher Tammy Thompson* took advantage of the opportunity to form an after school group called Praise Pals. However, she was discouraged from using her own classroom for the meetings in order to prevent the

*Name has been changed to protect privacy.

appearance of her leading the club in her official capacity as a teacher. Ms. Thompson could not use her instructional time to promote the group because of its religious nature. However, she could use other rooms in the school, just as other groups (i.e. Boy Scouts, churches, etc.) do. Furthermore, since the group was not an official, school-affiliated club, she could be free to play an active role in directing the activities. This was a role separate from that of being a teacher, and she was careful not to combine the two.

In Alaska, a Bible study was held at a teacher's home. It was a very small town, and many students, both from his class and from other classes, attended the Bible study. The principal was upset with the teacher even though he was doing nothing wrong. The law allows this type of activity because the teacher was not acting differently than any other citizen in the city, and he did not promote the study in his class. Despite the rather settled nature of the law, attorneys are still needed to intervene on some occasions. For example, in Santa Fe, New Mexico, a federal judge once ordered that teachers could not attend or participate in baccalaureate services. An attorney represented the teachers and immediately challenged the order before the 5th Circuit Court of Appeals, which reversed the judge's order as unconstitutional.[42]

Decorating your Classroom

Often, teachers are given discretion as to how they want their classrooms decorated. Teachers may wish to place on the walls of the classrooms positive character traits ("Don't Lie", "Don't Steal", or "Treat Others the Way You Wish to Be Treated"). Famous quotes from our nation's founding fathers, or copies of students' work on moral topics like "Why Honesty is Important" might be used. The teacher or principal might put up a display entitled, "The History and Development of American Law." Such a display might contain the Ten Commandments, Magna Carta, Declaration of Independence, United States Constitution, and the Bill of Rights.[43] (Note: Any attempt to put up *only* the Ten Commandments on school grounds would likely be challenged by the ACLU as an endorsement of religion.)

Teachers and Religious Harassment

Harassment is not okay just because a person has religious convictions. Title VII of the Civil Rights Act clearly mandates that employers reasonably accommodate the religious beliefs of their workers absent an undue burden on the employer. The same laws protecting against racial and gender harassment are generally just as applicable to cases of religious harassment. In your capacity as a teacher, if you are ordered to distribute material or if an assembly is announced that parents ought to be made aware of, you have a couple of viable options by which to approach this situation. First, you can ask for accommodation because of your religious beliefs. In doing so, you will not have to distribute objectionable material or attend an objectionable assembly. As a teacher, you have the right to make that request. For the teacher who cares about the students, the obvious problem with this solution is that the *students* then have to deal with the objectionable material or presentation.

Your second option is to attempt to send notice to parents. This may or may not be permitted by your principal. If it is, sending notice to parents about an objectionable assembly, for example, is the first step toward protecting the students and respecting the parents. After you send appropriate notice, you can offer to set up an alternative for students not attending the assembly. For example, any parent who objects to this particular assembly can ask that their children be sent to the library. As a teacher who also objects to the assembly, you can volunteer to watch over the students whom parents have requested be opted out. If the school's principal or superintendent does not allow teachers to contact parents before such presentations, the teacher is encouraged to contact the Pacific Justice Institute for immediate legal guidance.

Glenn's Story

Glenn Smith* did not think he was doing anything wrong, but he got into trouble anyway. He had a stellar record as a public school teacher for many years. After retiring from full-time teaching, Glenn decided he wanted to substitute. Again he had a great record as a substitute teacher. Why did this admirable teacher get in trouble? After substituting one day, he put the class records and notes together for the full-time teacher to see when she returned. At the bottom of the notes, he wrote a personal note that encouraged, complimented, and thanked the homeroom teacher for the pleasure of teaching her courteous and caring students. He also included a friendly holiday wish for the upcoming Easter holiday. That was it. That note was enough to upset

*Name has been changed to protect privacy

the teacher and cause the school administration to terminate Glenn. He was told he had made a religious comment to a teacher, which was deemed "inappropriate." Keep in mind that none of his comments were made known to the students. Did Glenn Smith just accept the punishment that will be on his record forever? No. Instead, he called the Pacific Justice Institute which took action on his behalf.

Teacher Not Forced to Choose Between Faith or Job

Laura Johnson* is an elementary teacher in Washington State. She was threatened with termination by her employer because of her need to have one hour off on Fridays due to her Messianic Jewish beliefs not to work past sundown on Fridays. Over the last school year her supervisor had accommodated her religious beliefs by allowing another employee to substitute for that hour. However, her new supervisor refused to provide her the same accommodation. Consequently, because the teacher was concerned that she may soon be terminated, Ms. Johnson contacted the Pacific Justice Institute. After receiving a demand letter from us, the employer reversed its position and agreed to accommodate the employee and allow her to take her hour off.

Teachers' Religious Rights Ignored

Several high school teachers in Hayward, California, were informed that they were required to attend an in-service staff development program that focuses on gay/lesbian/bi-sexual/transgender youth. On behalf of the teachers whose religious convictions disagree with the program's content, the Pacific Justice Institute petitioned the school's principal to accommodate the teachers by allowing them not to attend. The letter sent to the principal articulated the provisions of Title VII of the Civil Rights Act, which provides broad protections for people of religious faith in the workplace. As a teacher, if you are faced with a similar dilemma, please feel free to contact our office for assistance.

Remember, harassment is not okay just because the person harassed is a Christian. In fact, the same laws protecting against racial and gender harassment are generally just as applicable to cases involving religion. If you think the school administration or faculty is harassing you simply because of your religion, the Pacific Justice Institute is here to help you.

*Name has been changed to protect privacy

Choose Charity

What You Can Do With Your Union Dues

Depending on the area in which they live, many teachers find themselves paying and participating in a union without choice. Some teachers may want to be a part of their union to be salt and light and to make a difference. If God has called you to that, great! Do all you can to shine His light in this dark world. Often, however, teachers have religious convictions against supporting their unions. We find a lot of union members who are frustrated because they are forced to support unions which promote causes and candidates they believe are in opposition to God's Word. When talking with teachers and other union members about what they can do with their union dues, I am usually met with speculation. The questions are all the same. Surely they can have the political portions of their dues returned back to them, but what about the rest? There is nothing that can be done about the rest of the dues, is there? According to already existing law under Title VII, union members can have all — *yes I said ALL*— of their union dues given to a charity instead, if they are a religious objector to their union. Through a program developed by the Pacific Justice Institute called Choose Charity (www.pacificjustice.org), teachers and other union workers can inform the union of their religious objection to paying dues and ask to have the funds diverted to a mutually agreeable 501(c)(3) charity. You should be aware that under Federal Law, your union has the right to designate three charities for you to choose from when diverting your dues. If they do not designate any, then you may divert your dues to the nonprofit, non-labor, non-religious charity of your choice.

What Is Title VII and How Does it Help Me?

Title VII of the Civil Rights Act accommodates persons who object on religious grounds to the payment of union dues by allowing them to give to a charitable organization as a substitute form of payment. The courts have uniformly interpreted this provision to require accommodation through substitute charitable payments. In some instances, uncooperative unions have tried to discourage teachers from transferring their union dues to charities by demanding letters from clergy. The courts have ruled in favor of the employees ruling that they must thoroughly prove and explain why giving dues to the union is against their sincere religious beliefs, nothing more.

FAQ's about Donating Your Union Dues

You may have many questions about this process of diverting your union dues to charity. Because I have given this presentation a number of times to union members, we have noticed that many of the same questions are asked. Therefore, we have gathered a list of frequently asked questions so you can receive answers to some of the questions you may have.

What if my union will not let me donate my dues? What if they drill me about it?

Not only will they let you do this, they have to let you do this. It's the law. According to Title VII of the Civil Rights Act, they cannot require that you submit your church's doctrine for proof. You must merely establish the sincerity of your religious beliefs or convictions through an adequate explanation.

What about my union benefits? Will I still get my pay increase?

You will continue to receive any and all benefits of collective bargaining. You will keep the same pay as every member of the union, and receive the exact same benefits from your employer. However, if you do choose charity, you will lose your benefits provided directly by the union, such as extra liability insurance. In most instances, these benefits can be replaced at minimal cost by other organizations such as Christian Educators Association International (www.CEAI.org), and the Association of American Educators (www.aaeteachers.org).

What about the rest of my union dues? If the agency fee is the majority of my union dues, where is the rest of my money going?

If you are a "political objector" and do not want to join the union based on your political beliefs, then whatever money is not used for "agency fees" and instead goes toward the union's "political activity" can be returned to you.[44] No questions asked. Think of it; you would still technically have to pay your union dues, but some of it would come right back to you, and only the portion directly related to union representation would go to the union. As a "religious objector" who chooses not to join the union, based on religious beliefs, you have the right to divert the entire amount of your union dues to charity.[45]

What if I want to donate my dues to a political organization, like a specific party or political campaign?

Your dues can only be donated to a charity, not a political organization. If you have a specific organization in mind, but you are not sure if it qualifies, the best thing to do is to contact Pacific Justice Institute. We will assist you in any way we can.

I'm concerned about losing my union benefits. Can Pacific Justice Institute help me find ways to make up for those losses?

Absolutely. Pacific Justice Institute has a number of ways to supplement your benefits at a very low cost to you. Remember, you will keep any and all benefits from your employer and still benefit from collective bargaining.

Where do I send the letter requesting that my dues be given to a charity?

We have included a sample letter in the appendix in the back of this book (App 1). Feel free to use the language found in this letter, but do not copy it directly. After you have completed your letter, it is best to have someone at Pacific Justice Institute review it; therefore, we **request that you fax or email your letter to us.** After you get the green light from us, send it directly to your local union. They should know all about this provision and the process should be easy. If you have any questions, or if your union contacts you, please give us a call. We are here to help.

What if the union requests to see my church doctrine?

They can't require this. Two court decisions have declared a union member needs only to explain his/her sincere religious objection, and it does not have to be supported by any official church doctrine.[46] The employee simply has an obligation to provide a sufficient description of their religious belief or conviction to prove that it is in fact a sincere belief.[47] For example, you can quote religious scripture or discuss religious experiences (e.g., "God convicted me of . . .").

You may still have more questions about our Choose Charity Program. Please see App. 1, and then look up this program on our web site at www.pacificjustice.org. If you still have questions, please contact us, and we will help you in any way we can, free of charge. Choosing to reroute your union dues is just one of many ways you may choose to express your faith at your public school. (For additional information on teacher's rights, you may want to review a booklet titled "Teachers and Religions in Public Schools" by Kimberlee W. Colby, Esq. This booklet can be ordered at the Christian Educators Association International website: www.ceai.org).

5

WHAT'S A CHURCH TO DO?
Evangelism by Churches and Ministries

This section is most advantageous for youth ministers and directors of various evangelical ministries. Motivated students and parents will also find this section helpful and may want to pass it on to their youth ministers so that they might make the most of their legal opportunities to evangelize to public school students. Most religious people in our society see no possible opportunities for churches to evangelize effectively to public school students. On the contrary, opportunities for evangelism during, before and after school hours do exist.

Evangelism during School Hours

You may be surprised to know that very meaningful opportunities for churches and ministries to evangelize during school hours are available. Sadly, most churches either don't know about these opportunities or do not take advantage of them if they are aware of them. My wife Susanne, a former youth minister, will be the first to admit she had no idea what she was legally allowed to do in the public schools. That is part of our motivation in writing this book. We want other youth pastors to know what she did not know, and we want them to take advantage of these great opportunities.

RELEASED TIME PROGRAMS

Through the Lord's provision, I have had the opportunity to address a number of parents, church pastors, and teachers over the years. If we were to take a survey asking how many of them know what Released Time is, probably ninety percent would not know. Are you in the ten percent that does know?

Picture the following setting. It is nearing the last hour of the school day, and the teacher announces to the class that it is now time for children (whose parents have consented) to go to their Bible study class. Not only that, this announcement is made once every week during the entire school year. This may sound like a *Little House on the Prairie* rerun. In reality, it is exactly what can take place today in public school districts across the country through a program called Released Time. In order to pass constitutional scrutiny, the program must meet several requirements.

1) There can be no government funds expended for the program (i.e., printing consent forms for parents).

2) The program must be taught somewhere other than on school grounds (i.e., in a church, neighbor's house, or a bus parked across from the school).

3) Someone must teach the program other than one of the school's faculty.

4) The school must not promote the program, but it can send home information to parents along with information about other outside groups (e.g., soccer, Girl Scouts, etc.)[48]

States have passed laws allowing school districts to decide whether they want to allow such a program. Many school districts already have policies allowing for the program to operate. *According to surveys taken by Released Time organizations, a large number of students participating in Released Time make commitments to receive Christ by the end of the year.* Does this sound unbelievable to you? Check in your state, with your school district, to see what the law says about Released Time in your public schools. One state where Released Time education is very popular is Utah. The Mormon Church has taken full advantage of their religious freedom to spread their doctrine to children throughout the state. Christians can do the same. Remember, parental consent is necessary in order for children to participate in this program.

The Released Time Program will often take place on a Friday afternoon during the last hour of the day. So why don't most of America's elementary schools have this highly successful program? Many Americans and churches are either not aware or not willing to take advantage of this incredible opportunity. However, one church taking advantage of Released Time is Calvary Chapel. We encourage parents and pastors to look into Released Time as an exciting ministry opportunity. A number of organizations offer information on Released Time Programs, including California Released Time Christian Education (CRTCEA), Released Time Bible Classes, Inc., Fellowship of Christian Release Time Ministries, and BEST (Bible Education in School Time) Network, which is a national association of Released Time providers.

DEPOSITING RELIGIOUS BOOKS

I became a Christian when I was in third grade. Already an energetic and determined youngster, becoming a Christian made me even more zealous to make sure the right things were done. One day I discovered that my elementary school library did not have a Bible, but it did have Greek mythology books. Instead of accepting this as the way it was or simply complaining about it, I took action. (I guess my desire for justice and religious freedom began early in life!) I went to my library and asked the librarian if something could be done. In response, I filled out a request form for a Bible to be put in my school library, and as far as I know, it is still there today. (Note: It is usually much easier to request a book be placed in a library than it is to get one removed.)

Public school libraries have discretion as to what books they will decide to purchase for their school. However, a public school will often place some religious books in their library, especially if they are donated and the library already has some books of different religions. This is a tremendous opportunity for churches, parents, and even students to make a difference in their school.

Sometimes public schools will decide to set aside a location on campus for private individuals or businesses to donate books for children to pick up and read for free. One such high school decided to allow the Gideons to deposit Bibles at this location, along with other donated secular books. The ACLU filed suit against the school district.[49] (Is anyone surprised?) The federal district court ruled in favor of the school district solidifying another fantastic door of opportunity for religious reading material to be on an equal playing field with secular reading material. (Note: the district was required to put disclaimers on the Bibles so that there would be no confusion as to whether the school was endorsing religion), Similarly, PTA (Parent Teacher Association) book fairs generally may offer religious books along with secular books for sale to students.

PASTOR VISITATIONS

In a small town in San Joaquin Valley, California, a youth pastor was told that the school district's superintendent had made a decision regarding having pastors visit the school campus. He decided that clergy were no longer allowed to visit the children at school during lunchtime, even if the pastor had the parents' consent to do so. All other outsiders were not similarly restricted.

The Pacific Justice Institute contacted the superintendent to educate him on how, according to the law, the school district could not exclude only clergy from visiting the school campus. In response, the superintendent sent a letter stating that, because he could not solely exclude clergy, all outsiders were forbidden from visiting school grounds without the principal's consent. The school district soon recanted from this position after their attorney was enlightened as to the discriminatory purpose behind this seemingly non-discriminatory rule. Consequently, the youth pastor is still able to meet during lunchtime with those students whose parents have consented to such visits. However, if there is some resistance to your presence on campus, we encourage youth pastors not to visit so often that there is the alleged appearance of someone leading the Bible club other than the students.

You will find that almost every school has a different attitude toward youth pastors and workers visiting their school campus. Here, in her own words, is another account of an interesting school visitation my wife experienced:

> One of my interns and I had a very interesting time on one campus in Los Altos, California. When we first became involved with the Christian club at this high school, we were greeted with raised eyebrows and suspicion. We had to walk past a guard (an unhappy looking woman) into the fenced school, and she would question us about whether or not we had permission to be there. She would do this month after month (we

56

visited every one to two months) even though she recognized us from the previous times we visited. Then the Columbine High School shooting tragedy occurred in Colorado. Everything changed. It is considered the most horrific school shooting in history, and one that will stay in our memories forever. The day after the Columbine shooting, my intern and I headed to the high school in Los Altos to speak to the Christian club. The usual guard was there, but this time, instead of the raised eyebrow, she actually greeted us with a tentative smile. She said she was glad to see us, and she was grateful we were there because the school needed it. We were amazed! Sometimes, though, it takes something like what happened at Columbine for people to realize how far off track the world has gone. All of a sudden the people who are tentative, possibly even hostile to religion before, realize that for students to learn right and wrong and the Ten Commandments isn't such a bad thing after all.

This experience that Susanne shared is not an uncommon one, according to her friends who are also involved in youth ministry. We do not, however, need tragedies to change the tide of school visitations. The general rule is if schools have opened their campus to visits by non-faculty adults during lunchtime, the school will likely find it difficult to exclude clergy. Youth pastors should take advantage of this opportunity to spend time with their students during lunch and at Bible clubs, which generally meet during lunchtime.

Evangelism Before or After School Hours

Of all areas of evangelism in public schools, evangelism by churches and outside organizations is probably one of the most neglected. The reason for the neglect is simple. Many are not aware of the legal opportunities that exist for churches to minister on school campuses. What kind of activities or programs could a church or para-church ministry implement or participate in after school hours at a public school? The potential list is almost as broad as the imagination will take it. Nonetheless, we list below a few tested ideas.

CHURCH LEASING OF SCHOOL FACILITIES

Many are not aware of the fact that when a school allows non-religious outside groups to use or lease its facilities after school hours, it generally cannot discriminate against other outside organizations simply because of their religious purpose or backing. For example, if a school allows Cub Scouts to meet after school, it cannot prohibit AWANAS (a religious organization) from having the same opportunity. Similarly, the 4th Circuit Court of Appeals ruled that schools couldn't make a profit by making a religious organization pay more rent than any other non-religious organization.[50]

School Board Rejects Proposal to Charge Churches More

A school district in Northern California voted to reject a proposal that would increase the rates religious institutions have to pay to lease school facilities. Under the existing proposal, churches, like other non-profit organizations, only have to pay the direct costs incurred by the school resulting from the church's use of their facilities. The rejected proposal would have treated churches differently by requiring them to pay a higher rate than other non-profit organizations. The Pacific Justice Institute intervened in the matter on behalf of a local church and provided a statutory and constitutional analysis on the proposal.

Many opportunities are available to churches that lease school facilities. Susanne's home church in Rowland Heights, California, used to meet in an elementary school. While many churches get discouraged about meeting in a school for a long period of time, many ministry opportunities have opened up as a result of their location. Each year the church provided Christmas meals and presents to a minimum of fifty needy families in the school district. The church also organized an alternative Harvest Carnival on October 31st on school grounds. The event was highly successful because it provided a safe alternative to Halloween in a familiar setting to families. Churches leasing a school facility are utilizing just one of the many ways in which churches can minister before or after school hours.

REVIVAL RALLIES

This is by far one of the most dynamic methods of campus evangelism, and yet one of the least used. Just imagine your church equipped with the legal right to come on school grounds right after school hours and put on a revival rally in the elementary, junior high, or high school gymnasium! A Christian band plays exciting music. Ex-gay and ex-drug users share their testimonies. A youth minister gives an altar call! Based upon the law discussed in Chapter 3, there is virtually no reason why your local public schools cannot be impacted in this way. However, there is one caution . . . a church deciding to put on one of these rallies may witness an *explosion* in their youth programs! We at the Pacific Justice Institute look forward to equipping every single youth minister, youth ministry, or group of students wishing to turn this scenario into a complete reality. **(Because Susanne and I feel this is so important, we decided to include the discussion of revival rallies in two different chapters!)**

THE 5TH QUARTER (after football and basketball games)

Similar to revival rallies, 5th Quarter events occur right after a football game or other sporting event. They can be held in the school gym or other large facility at the school. This is a great opportunity to minister to the students from one particular school. Selected clips of the games can be shown to the students while they munch down pizza. In this environment youth workers can share spiritually with the participating students in a manner maybe not as intense as the revival rally, but possibly just as effective. Holding an event like this at a local school can be very effective in reaching *new* students. However, if your youth ministry has a number of students from a variety of schools, you may decide to hold a similar event at your own church gym or large multi-purpose room.

My wife and I attended a Business Men's Fellowship Conference in the Bay area. Part of the evening program included a group called the Power Team. The Team showed off their muscles by lifting heavy items and breaking bricks and thick boards with their bare hands! They also "showed off" their faith in the Lord and gave inspiring testimonies of Christ working in their lives. Groups such as this one put on presentations that combine interesting shows with positive and inspirational messages. Having one of these groups at your event could really be a powerful way to minister to many young people.

BIBLE STUDY/PRAISE GROUPS

As mentioned before in our section for teachers, Ms. Tammy Thompson started such a group after school hours at her elementary school. The children would sing, learn from the Bible, do crafts, and play positive, value-oriented games. As long as the school allows other outside groups to use their facility,[51] the general rule is that they cannot exclude similar student-oriented religious groups (e.g. AWANAS). Churches and ministries can use school grounds to organize a Bible study group before and after school hours. There are generally no limits as long as the event is sponsored and organized by the church.

ATHLETIC PROGRAMS

Sometimes, when a school district has to cut its budget, after school athletic programs are often at the top of the list to be eliminated or drastically cut. In addition, teachers' unions will often refuse to allow members to serve as after-school athletic coaches without pay. Consequently, it is not uncommon for after-school athletic voids to exist.

Fortunately, for many Houston inner-city youths, a number of churches decided to fill that void by implementing athletic programs geared toward not just keeping children occupied, but also toward teaching them principles to last a lifetime. Starting an athletic ministry in your church and requesting to use the school's facility is a great way to reach out to young people today. You can also work together with other churches (like they did in Houston) to put together an after-school athletic program that really ministers to the youth. Another idea is for the youth pastor and/or youth workers in the church to volunteer to coach after-school athletic programs. An excellent resource to contact for sports ministry information is the Fellowship of Christian Athletes (See website list in the back of this book.)

TUTORING PROGRAMS

Many children, for whatever reason, do not receive the tutorial assistance needed from either the public school or their parents. This leaves a tremendous void to be filled by individual churches or organizations. For example, St. Luke's Lutheran Church decided to adopt just one particular school in their community to begin a tutorial program. Since the program may, in fact, have a religious slant (i.e. prayer, scriptural encouragement, etc.) the church cannot expect the school to promote or financially support the program in any way. However, the church is generally still entitled to use the school facility (i.e. a classroom) after school hours just like any other outside after-school group. Also, the local PTA (Parent/Teacher Association) could announce the tutoring program to parents along with other local tutorial programs. Such constructive church involvement refutes the attempts of those who want to paint many evangelical churches as the enemy of public schools. We know of one community, San Bernardino, California, that has aggressively risen to this challenge. A group of their local pastors visit the schools frequently to serve the students as mentors and tutors.

BACCALAUREATE SERVICES

A baccalaureate service is one that honors students graduating from school, yet inherently has a religious emphasis to it. Because many schools have attempted to restrict the use of religious speech during graduation ceremonies, churches and parents have begun to organize these services as an addition to the graduation ceremony. As governmental establishments, courts may attempt to restrict public high schools from organizing religious baccalaureate services in the future. However, parents and churches may sponsor a baccalaureate service either at their church or at a high school after school hours. (See App. 3) As long as the high school has allowed (or as in some states, is required to allow) other outside groups to use its facilities after school, it may not discriminate against parents or churches simply because their purposes are religious.[52] Furthermore, a student-initiated Bible club may also sponsor a baccalaureate service and advertise it along with its other school events by placing posters in designated areas of the school. The schools announcing the club-sponsored baccalaureate services in school publications are merely accommodating religious practices and not endorsing them. In addition, it is legal for students to pass out flyers about the baccalaureate service as long as advertising efforts do not disrupt class.

ACTIVITIES ON CHURCH GROUNDS

While some churches, for various reasons, may feel reluctant to orchestrate activities on school grounds, there exist tremendous opportunities to conduct before and after-school programs on church grounds. For example, it is fairly common for Mormons to conduct early morning educational activities at their church where, after the activity, the students are often picked up by a school bus and taken to school. Mormons have also frequently built their churches right across from school grounds to make such instruction easily accessible. Christian churches could easily replicate this model.

In the same way, churches could function as after-school centers of activity for elementary, junior high and high school students. Such programs have become increasingly popular as America continues to increase its two-income or one-parent households. These programs provide both a safe alternative plus an evangelical outreach tool to the many who, in the past, have been complacent toward churches. In fact, the Pacific Justice Institute has provided counsel to churches establishing not only after-school programs, but also day care centers!

Getting the Information Out

Many attempting to start a school program or event often wonder how they can make the students' parents aware of it. Schools may pass out information on these programs along with other non-religious after school programs (i.e. Boy Scouts, soccer clubs, etc.), as long as the information does not convey the semblance of state endorsement. The PTA may include information about these programs in their newsletters to parents. Flyers may be handed out to students on the outside public sidewalk in front of the school. Flyers may also be hand delivered to local residences surrounding the particular school. If the school allows other outside organizations to have copies of the names and addresses of the students' parents (many do not for security reasons), the school could possibly be forced to enable the religious organization to have the same access.

Above all, the most effective method of getting information to children or teenagers is by having them distribute this information directly to their peers, before or after school, or during lunch or recess. The bottom line is simply this: If a church or religious organization wants to get a program started, there are plenty of ways available to do so and to keep students and parents informed.

6

BUT I'M JUST A PARENT!
Opportunities for Parents to Evangelize and Protect their Children

Listen to Your Kids and Take Action

Someone once said, "The only thing worse than being in a war is being in a war and not knowing it." This phrase rings true for many cases involving parents. We are in the midst of a culture war involving our children, and parents must realize that, in a war, casualties occur. Our goal as an organization is to minimize and eventually eradicate those casualties. Your goal as parents is to prevent your children from being one of the casualties of this culture war.

Many of our cases involving parents and schools come as a result of child/parent communication. If children are comfortable talking to their parents about what is happening at their school, and parents take the time to listen, much can be accomplished.

School District Reverses to Allow Christmas Play

The Pacific Justice Institute was contacted by parents from East Bay, California, who learned that their elementary school would not allow for the Christmas program to take place because of the alleged "separation of church and state." One of our in-house attorneys immediately sent the parents a legal opinion letter explaining that such presentations are constitutional since they are only teaching about a religious holiday and not proselytizing a particular faith. The school soon reversed their position and agreed to allow the Christmas production to take place.

As you have read throughout this book, parents take a lot of action to protect their children and their children's religious freedom. God has given us children to raise and protect. It is our job, not the school's, to make the final determination of what our kids should and should not learn. Courts have held that parents have a fundamental right over their children.[53] That fundamental right is essential for enabling parents to exercise the responsibility of parenting that God has given them. One time Brad was speaking before a school board and a group of parents. A debate was ensuing and a local representative from the California Teachers Association (CTA) stood up and said, "Do you mean to tell me that you think that parents know better what is best for their kids than educational experts in Sacramento?" As the parents sat, shocked into silence, Brad quickly thanked the representative for so clearly stating what the perspective of the CTA was—*that parents do not actually know what is best for their children.* As we discussed the concept for this book, one of our goals was to make you, as parents, aware of some ways you can protect your children, be involved with your schools, take action, and evangelize in the parental position in which God has placed you.

You Can Protect Your Children

It may sound strange, and a bit sad, that we are encouraging you to protect your children in the public school. The truth is, our public schools have changed dramatically in recent years. Parents used to send their children to school confident in its ability to teach correctly and objectively, without bias to one social agenda over another. Times have changed; it is now time for parents to take the necessary steps to protect their children in public schools. One way this can be done is by keeping an opt-out form on file with the school. This opt-out form, described later in this chapter, enables a parent to opt their child out of controversial curriculum or presentations. *Parents ought to also keep a letter from a certified counselor on file at their child's school.* The purpose of this letter, which should be stated in writing by the parent, is to ensure that no counseling can occur at school without a call to the student's personal counselor because of personal and spiritual implications. The past years of defending parents' rights and religious freedoms have provided us with a glimpse of how the world of public schools has changed. It is vital that parents become aware of all that is going on in their child's school.

Parents Object to New Age Song Presented to Kindergarten Class

The parents of a Kindergarten student in California were shocked after learning their daughter's Kindergarten class was forced to listen to, and participate in, a New Age song while on a field trip. The song, which the parents consider Wicca/New Age, included lyrics that they found extremely inappropriate. The class was on a forestry field trip relating to ecosystems curriculum, and at some point, the students were handed a song sheet. At the top of the page were the words, *"Where I sit is holy. Holy is the ground. Forest, mountains, river—listen to the sound. Great spirits circle all around me."* The lyrics continued as follows: *"Ancient Mother, I hear you calling, Ancient Mother, I hear your song. Ancient Mother, I hear your laughter, Ancient Mother, I taste your tears. O la mama wa ha su kay la, O la mama wa ha su om, O la mama ka way ha ha ha ha, O la mama ta te ka kay. So be it."*

We know this may sound hard to believe, but trust us, this story is true. The parents objected to their child's exposure to the lyrics without prior parental notice. [Note that the 9th Circuit Court of Appeals may not find this activity to be unconstitutional.][54] The parents contacted us at the Pacific Justice Institute and we assisted them in filing a complaint with the school district.

Parent-based Organizations Take Action

In addition to individual parents, parent-based, grass roots organizations can play an enormous role as well. For example, in Fresno, CA, the school district was delayed in showing a sexually crude theatrical presentation after being informed that they had failed to provide parents adequate legal prior notice of the event. Parents involved in the local Concerned Women for America (see website list) chapter took advantage of the delay, rallied the community, and the presentation was canceled altogether. Similarly a local chapter of Eagle Forum (see website list) in Santa Rosa, CA, rallied parents to push for drastic school district policy changes. The rallying followed the filing of an administrative complaint by the Pacific Justice Institute after a school had once again failed to give adequate notice of another sexually crude presentation.

The moral of the story: Along with the legal representation provided by the Pacific Justice Institute, there often exist local grass root organizations that can provide valuable support to parents as well.

BE AWARE

As we travel around the country, especially in California, one of the questions most commonly asked by parents is: "But what can I do to protect my children once they are in school?" Parents often experience a sense of helplessness once they send their children (of all ages) into the classroom. The above story is just one example of what you can do to protect your children. Be aware of all that is going on with your children both at school and at school related events, including field trips and assemblies.

Public Schools Peddle Book Promoting Witchcraft

An elementary school in Utah was caught peddling a book to elementary school students entitled, "The Wizards Handbook." The Scholastic Book Club order form promotes the book by stating, "Find the Wizard Inside YOU!" and "Make your own magic wands, cast spells, predict the future, and lots more!" A concerned parent contacted us after learning the school was making available such a book to her child, without any prior parental notice or consent. After reviewing the matter, Roger Ho, a Pacific Justice Institute attorney, sent a legal demand letter to the superintendent of the school district. "By encouraging the students to purchase the handbook, the school is effectively encouraging the adoption of certain religious practices normally identified with witchcraft-based religions," said Mr. Ho. "Since the religious text is not being offered for literary or historic value, and no other religious book is being offered, the school is running a risk of violating the First Amendment's Establishment Clause." The Superintendent of the school district chose to resolve the matter by no longer allowing the book to be sold at the school.

School Invites Planned Parenthood without Parental Notice

As a freshman at Arcata High School in Arcata, California, taking health class is a requirement as part of the curriculum. As part of the course outline, school administrators invited guest speakers from Planned Parenthood to address the class of freshmen. The topic to be covered by Planned Parenthood was sexual education, but more specifically "homophobia" and homosexuality. The school administrators who invited Planned Parenthood to the class failed to give prior notice to parents, and the school did not obtain parental written consent for this presentation.

As part of an icebreaker, Planned Parenthood asked the class to stand in a circle. Questions were then asked of the class regarding "homophobia" and homosexuality. Whenever a question was asked that applied to the students, the students were asked by Planned Parenthood to step into the middle of the circle, facing their peers. One question was, "Does your religion believe against or think homosexuality is a sin or something wrong?" Feeling humiliated and singled out, only a few students stepped forward. "This made me feel very uncomfortable," claimed one of the freshman students. "I felt like I was being judged as a bad person… my classmates stared at me like I had done something wrong."

This line of questioning is tantamount to religious-based harassment and violates both state and federal law when it is performed without prior written parental consent. Events like this can slip "under the radar" if, as a parent, you are unaware of what is happening in your child's school. Unfortunately, as evidenced by this true story, religious-based harassment can occur even if one *does* take steps to be aware. On behalf of the aforementioned student, the Pacific Justice Institute agreed to offer any legal assistance and represent parents throughout the administrative complaint process. This was such a "hot topic" of discussion, the O'Reilly Factor on Fox News Channel asked Brad to come on the program to explain what happened. If you or your children face such harassment, please contact our office.

Pacific Justice Institute believes in preserving the rights of parents over their children. We are committed to preserving those rights. However, it is up to each and every parent to be aware of what his/her child is exposed to in their public school. We have some advice to help you protect your children from both objectionable classroom material and assemblies or presentations.

OPT-OUT FORMS

Filling out an opt-out form and giving it to your school enables you to opt your child or children out of certain subjects, projects or assemblies with which you disagree. For those parents in California, we have an opt-out form that was put together by the Pacific Justice Institute. This form can be found in Appendix 1 and can be copied to be used for all of your children or to be distributed to other parents. However, if you are *outside* of California, please contact Pacific Justice Institute's Legal Department for assistance. After filling out your form(s), we encourage you to 1.) Mail a copy to our office: P.O. Box 276600, Sacramento, CA 95827 2.) Personally give a copy to your child's principal and teachers, and 3.) Keep a copy for yourself.

Sacramento School Finally Accommodates Parent's Opt-Out Request

A mother with a son attending a high school in a Sacramento school district was outraged to learn that her son's teacher used classroom time to advocate moral acceptance of homosexuality. The mother contacted the Pacific Justice Institute who provided her with an opt-out form and advised the mother how to have her child placed with a different teacher. At first, the principal refused to agree with the parental request, but after receiving the parents' letter and conferring with the teacher, the son was finally placed in an alternative classroom. The school district allegedly has begun a "tolerance" program, which was initially used to justify the teacher's remarks.

Does this form ensure that you will never have problems with your child seeing and/or hearing objectionable material? Sadly, we have had to deal with a couple of school districts who have "lost" or "misplaced" a number of these forms at the time of a *highly* objectionable assembly. We are dealing with those school districts on a legal level now. However, do not let that discourage you. Even if the form is "lost" or ignored, the fact that it was filed puts the parents in a much stronger bargaining and legal position.

REVIEW YOUR CHILDREN'S CURRICULM

As a parent you have every right to review your children's textbooks before the beginning of the year. This is highly recommended because of the rise of revisionist history and homosexual language in changing textbooks. Just call your child's school during the summer to request a review of the textbooks. You should be able to take these textbooks home so you can take your time to review them carefully. The following is an outrageous example of what can happen when we close our eyes to the curriculum young people are being taught in public schools.

Islam Takes Over Middle School Curriculum

A class of seventh graders begins the class with their teacher taking attendance: "Ali Muhammad?" "Here." "Abdul Muhammad Ishmael?" "Here." Then the class gets on its knees, and the students lower their heads to the floor. Some students are given extra credit for memorizing verses from the Quran. Where is their class located? Iraq? Iran? Saudi Arabia? No, try California.

A mother was outraged to find out that the school district in San Luis Obispo was causing her seventh grade son to feel very uncomfortable about the Islamic-based curriculum being taught to him. She brought the above incident to our attention in December 2001. When the school district refused to allow the mother to opt her child out of the instruction, she contacted us at the Pacific Justice Institute. We then investigated and discovered that the teacher used a specific textbook designed to help teachers lead these Muslim simulations. Several lawsuits are pending over the use of this textbook in the public school system.

As a result of this investigation, the Pacific Justice Institute discovered that, although the activities varied from school to school, nearly every seventh grade class in California used the textbook, *Across the Centuries*, which was also filled with the pro-Islamic, anti-Christian propaganda. The state-endorsed textbook used by the teachers puts the history of the Islamic faith in a purely positive light, while depicting Christians in a negative light. We have since assisted a number of parents in California in filing administrative complaints with their school districts as well as representing them in their requests to opt their children out of the highly controversial instruction.

Although it is not unconstitutional for schools to teach about different religions, established case law requires that such instruction be neither hostile nor preferential toward any particular faith. In other words, religious instruction must be balanced. So how "balanced" is *Across the Centuries*? Page sixty-four portrays Islam as giving women "rights of their own," yet the textbook conveniently forgets to mention how Islam allows a male adherent to have four wives (and not vice-versa). Other portions of the textbook refer to statements of belief as statements of fact. *"In fact, the very first word the Angel Gabriel spoke to Muhammad was 'recite',"* according to page 63 of the text. In describing Muhammad, the textbook makes no mention of the fact that Muhammad not only owned slaves, but also was an active slave trader. The textbook also attempts to downplay his role as a warrior leading numerous battles in a holy Jihad against alleged infidels. Instead it states, on page 65, that *"Muhammad's success in spreading Islam was due in large part to his strong character, morality, courage and compassion".* When it discusses why Jerusalem is so important to different religions, page 280 of the textbook Across the Centuries says that: *"Jerusalem is where Jesus was crucified and buried, and it was where Muhammad rose to heaven."*

Is the word "resurrection" too difficult to spell? The book actually states: "the Muslims treated Christians and Jews with such tolerance that some converted to Islam or at least adopted many of its customs." Nowhere in the text does it refer to Christians being tolerant of other people. According to Brian Mitchell's article in "Investors Business Daily": *"They are said to have persecuted Jews 'often' and 'without mercy.' They are said to have persecuted their own people, causing some to 'welcome Muslim rule.'"* Mitchell also states: *"Certain things about Muslims and Christians get said over and over again, so the student can't help but remember them, after the facts in between are forgotten."*

On page 315 of the first edition under the caption "Understanding Religious Persecution", the textbook only refers to how Christians persecuted people of other faiths. (Note: These are just a few of the many examples of bias and propaganda reflected in this book.) By far, the greatest controversy comes from supplemental material found by an Associated Press Reporter for the San Francisco Examiner. This reporter found classroom handouts stating: "You and your classmates will become Muslims. The student assumes a Muslim name, wears Muslim clothes, and even memorizes a prayer that includes the line, 'Praise be to Allah, Lord of Creation.'"

This example of biased curriculum being taught in California is just one of many that parents ought to be aware of. We at the Pacific Justice Institute are currently representing parents to contest this clear abridgement of parental trust. Our hope is that public education remembers that its primary duty is to educate and not indoctrinate.

ASK YOUR SCHOOL BOARD TO FORM A PARENTAL REVIEW COMMITTEE

An even more proactive approach is convincing your school board to form a parental review committee to approve all new textbooks and library books. A number of school districts have already begun to adopt such policies. Reviewing textbooks and curriculum thoroughly is time-consuming, whether it is done individually or as a committee. However, knowing what our children are being taught makes it worth whatever effort is necessary.

Sexually Graphic Books Assigned to Ninth Graders

In response to the actions of parents and the Pacific Justice Institute, the school board and principal of Colusa High School in California responded swiftly and decisively to parental complaints regarding inappropriate reading assignments given to ninth graders. Five objectionable and inappropriate books were removed from the school's approved reading list. In March and April of 2002, ninth grade students were given reading lists from which to choose books for their co-ed literacy discussion groups. Students' parents were shocked and outraged when they discovered that many of the books contained abundant profanity, graphic sexual and homosexual content, violence and drugs. When confronted, the school initially responded that the books were on the American Library Association's Recommended Reading List for young adults.

At the request of one of the involved parents, the Pacific Justice Institute immediately prepared an opinion letter that one mother was able to take to the School Board meeting. The Colusa Unified School Board responded to the parent's complaints and apologized for the inappropriate book list that had been given to the students. The School Board also stated it was establishing a book review committee. The Institute also confirmed that at least four of the removed books were named in the American Library Association's "Best Books for Young Adults" list in both 1998 and 2000.

This outrageous example is just one of many that can be found in public schools today. Whatever you decide to do, always remember that the greatest way to protect your children is to be aware of what is going on in their school and classrooms, *starting with the books they will read.* Due to an overwhelming response from concerned parents regarding the Colusa school case, we have decided to include the titles of the books mentioned in this and previous cases. We are also including other books to look out for found in the Focus on the Family *Love Won Out* booklet. These books include:

Inappropriate Books:
A Beach Party with Alexis: A Coloring Book
A Boy's Best Friend
Across the Centuries (textbook)
A History of Western Society (textbook)
Always Running
Am I Blue?
Anna-Day and the O-Ring
Annie on My Mind
Asha's Mums
Athletic Shorts
Bad by Jean Ferris
Becoming Visible
Belinda's Bouquet
Commitment and Love
Daddy's Roommate
Entries from a Hot Pink Notebook
Families: A Celebration of Diversity
Families: A Coloring Book
Gloria Goes to Gay Pride
Heather Has Two Mommies
How Would You Feel If Your Dad Was Gay?
Imani All Mine by Connie Porter
Invisible Life
Jenny Lives With Eric and Martin
Just As I Am
*My Two Uncle*s
One Dad, Two Dads, Brown Dads, Blue Dads
Saturday is Pattyday
Tenderness by Robert Cormier
The Daddy Machine
The Day They Put a Tax on Rainbows and Other Stories
The Duke Who Outlawed Jelly Beans
The Entertainer
The Generous Bartleby Jones

BECOME A VOLUNTEER

The loudest complainers are often the ones who take the least amount of action. One of the best ways to know what is going on in your child's school is to volunteer in your child's class. If you have some frustrations with the public school system or are concerned about its impact on young people, especially your own, become a volunteer either in your child's class or in another. You can also become our eyes and ears and contact us if you observe any questionable activities or curriculum.

Teacher Forced To Halt Native American Religious Rituals

Due to the objections of parents, a fourth grade school teacher at an elementary school in California halted the religious Native American rituals she was performing in her classroom. These rituals included the use of a medicine wheel and morning chants where she addressed the north, south, east, and west, along with father heaven and mother earth. The ritual also involved the burning of sage in the classroom in conjunction with the daily recitation. She later replaced the sage with a rattle. In Shamanism, a rattle is used during prayer to announce one's intention to the spirits in each of the four cardinal directions. A concerned parent notified us of the outrageous conduct and religious ritual practices after the school district refused to respond to her complaints. The Pacific Justice Institute sent a detailed demand letter to the school district's legal counsel making it clear that such activity was an unconstitutional violation of the rights of families with traditional religious beliefs. The law firm informed the Institute that the teacher would no longer continue such practices.

Becoming a volunteer in your child's classroom would help derail unconstitutional activities such as the case you just read. If you cannot volunteer in your child's classroom, think about volunteering in the school office. If you are able to do this, you can observe upcoming events and be "in the know" on issues that many parents do not know anything about.

If you cannot volunteer on a consistent basis in the classroom or school office, other options still exist. You can volunteer to help with school plays or assemblies. Volunteering during special events and participating in PTA and Board meetings will also contribute to your knowledge of what is happening at your child's school.

ASK FOR A COMPLETE SCHEDULE OF EVENTS

All schools provide a variety of extra activities and events other than the usual classroom time. These events often include field trips, theme weeks, and special assemblies. It is important for you to ask your child's school for a *complete* schedule of events including details regarding speakers and themes. If you have any questions regarding a particular event, feel free to call the school and ask for more details. Remember, this is **your** child, and you have **every** right to know what he or she is being taught and exposed to during school hours.

"Week of Diversity" Catches Parents off Guard

In Northern California some parents called their local high school to see what the upcoming "week of diversity" would entail. The "week of diversity" began with an assembly dealing with sexuality issues that parents thought was not appropriate for the students. The assembly called "Sex and Stuff" included vulgar, inappropriate sex scenes, and recommended alternative sex acts instead of abstinence. Also discussed were topics such as sexual molestation, rape, unwanted pregnancy, and HIV. The school conducted this assembly after parents had explicitly made it clear through an opt-out form that their children were not supposed to participate in any activities during a "Week of Diversity." The parents had been given a schedule of *seminars* for the week. *The materials sent to parents did not include any mention of the general assembly, or its questionable content.* After Pacific Justice Institute threatened to sue the school district, the district gave in to the reforms demanded by the parents.

It is important for you to ask for a *complete* schedule of events. Do not simply trust that an upcoming assembly will be appropriate for the students. Again, if you become a volunteer, you will be aware of upcoming events such as the one that happened in the Northern California school.

All Children Matter

While opt-out forms are recommended, remember that the rest of the students are exposed to the objectionable material unless: 1) You make sure that all parents are given the option of opting their child out, or 2) You contact the Pacific Justice Institute to inform our staff of the concerns you have about the upcoming school curriculum or assembly. Every parent's first responsibility is to our children; they are a gift from God. However, keep in mind that there are so many children being exposed to that which is evil and/or damaging to their lives. Please help us get the word out to as many parents as possible about our opt-out forms and about our willingness to help them in time of need.

BE AWARE OF THE LAW

We have laws in this country for a reason. Knowing these laws will help you protect your children. For example, states (e.g., California) often require prior notice to parents or written parental consent for sex education, HIV/AIDS education, or surveys containing questions about sex, morality, family life, or religion. If your child's school has engaged in such presentations or taken surveys dealing with one or more of these issues without your notice or consent, they may have broken the law, and you can take action.[55] If you suspect that this is the case in your child's school, feel free to call the Pacific Justice Institute to see what the law says on that particular issue. If the answer is not immediately known, the in-house attorneys can do research to find the answer to your question. In addition, knowing what the law says also equips you to proactively evangelize your public schools.

ORGANIZE AN INFORMATIONAL MEETING

An effective way of making a difference is to mobilize parents at your school and church for a meeting. Invite one of our attorneys to speak to parents about their rights and what they should watch for in their school. Providing an organized meeting along with a question and answer time will give parents more confidence when dealing with the public school system. Knowing they have the assistance of Pacific Justice Institute, an organization willing to help and defend without charge, will enable some parents to take stands that they might not have taken otherwise.

OFFER MODEL POLICIES TO YOUR SCHOOL BOARD

Even a "hostile" school board usually has at least one member who is willing to listen to parents. Set up a meeting with that board member and ask him or her to consider sponsoring one or more of the model policies we have listed in the next chapter.

Evangelism Opportunities

As a parent you can make a difference in the lives of public school teachers, students and staff. We have listed some ways in which you can take advantage of the opportunities God has made available to you.

GET TO KNOW THE STAFF AND TEACHERS

Life is so busy that we do not often take the time to know the people our children see daily. The employees at your children's school communicate with them on a daily basis. Getting to know the staff, administrators, and especially your child's teacher will not only help to protect your children, but will also provide opportunities for you to share your faith. Because public school employees are cautious not to display their faith inappropriately or in a manner that might violate the law, it may take a few visits or conversations before you can determine the religious or non-religious views of the staff at your public school. Take advantage of where God has placed you as a parent by getting to know them for the purpose of protection and constructive evangelism.

RUN FOR SCHOOL BOARD

You may have heard the phrase, "Making a difference begins with local politics." There is a lot of truth to that statement, especially concerning your school district and the decisions made by your school board. Your local school board makes important decisions for the many children and teenagers who attend public schools. We need more Christians on school boards. Think about running for your school board by yourself or consider getting a couple of people to join you and run as a team, a very effective strategy.

BECOME A SUBSTITUTE OR CREDENTIALED SCHOOL TEACHER

As mentioned earlier, we never want to give good public school teachers the impression that their decision to teach is a bad one. Actually, we need more good teachers and Christian teachers to make an impact in the lives of young people today. Becoming a credentialed or substitute teacher is an effective way to meet a number of students who need the encouragement and guidance of adults who really care about their welfare.

VOLUNTEER FOR A TEACHER

In the previous section we mentioned volunteering as a great way to protect your children. Becoming a volunteer will also provide you with a great opportunity to get to know a teacher in a unique way that is not always possible when you are simply a parent. It will also give you access to students with whom you can share encouragement and the love of Christ by your example.

PRAY FOR TEACHERS

At Sunrise Community Church in Fair Oaks, California, Pastor Rich Sherman shared a story about praying for his children's teachers. When he and his wife would attend parent/teacher conferences, he would let the teacher know that he and his wife were praying for them. He said the teachers would often get emotional and one teacher said, "I didn't know *anyone* prayed for me." What an incredible ministry opportunity Christians have in the form of prayer. Parents ought to be dedicated in prayer for their children's teachers and for any other teacher God puts on their heart.

PRAY FOR AND MENTOR STUDENTS

According to a mentoring ministry called *One Kid at a Time*, thirty percent of children today have no father active in their life, the divorce rate has doubled since 1970, and one-third of all births are to unmarried mothers. It is not surprising that prayers should extend to students also, whether friends of your children or simply a child the Lord puts on your heart. Praying plus mentoring is a very effective means of ministering to young people today. Just one or two hours a week can make a world of difference in the development of a child who may have no fatherly role model. If the Lord puts it on your heart to do so, make a commitment to mentor and pray for at least one student in your local public school. For help in this area of ministry, contact *One Kid at a Time*. (See website list.)

BE A CRITICAL MOBILIZER WITH YOUR YOUTH PASTOR

You can work with your child's youth pastor to help organize Christian clubs and revival rallies. Youth pastors can always use the help of volunteers to make calls, develop flyers, and help organize events that pull youth in from the public school. Your greatest task may be in making your youth pastor aware of the tremendous opportunities he or she has to reach out to students at public schools. Now that you have read this book, you can let him or her know about all of these exciting *and legal* opportunities. You can also let your youth pastor know that Pacific Justice Institute is here to help if he or she runs into any problems in attempting to start Christian clubs and revival rallies. Furthermore, you can make your youth pastor aware of valuable ministries specializing in youth outreach, including (but not limited to), Christ in Youth, Young Life, Campus Crusade, and Youth for Christ. (See email list.)

In order to make a difference you first must be aware of the problem. As mentioned earlier, being involved in your children's school will aid you in that process. Another way to do so, which is gaining popularity, is working with your pastor to organize a church committee that makes itself aware of upcoming laws and concerns that may affect parents and the church. This type of committee can be called the Pastor's Information Resource Council (PIRC). Emmanuel Baptist Church in Highland, California, has done an excellent job of putting together such a committee. We consider them the experts and encourage you to look up their website which is included in the back of our book. Consider bringing this idea up to your pastor; however, be willing to take on the responsibility if you are asked to.

Considering Educational Options

While the focus of this book is on the opportunity and freedom for evangelism in public schools, we thought it important to include a few schooling options in existence, other than traditional public schools. Depending on the area in which you live and the quality (or lack thereof) of your local public school, you may be seriously considering changing your child's schooling. This section provides a brief overview of schooling options and offers a reminder of the important educational decisions for which parents are responsible.

OUR SCHOOLING BACKGROUND

Before we discuss the various schooling options that are available today, it is important that we share with you some of our background. I attended private school most of my life. One reason for this is that my parents were not pleased with the conditions in the local public school. After high school I chose to go to a private Christian college so I could major in Christian Education. Brad, on the other hand, attended *public* school all of his life, including undergraduate and law school. He was pleased with how attending public school prepared him for what he is doing now. That said, he is actually quite a strong proponent of private and home schooling. The reasons for this are actually quite simple. Public schools have dramatically changed since he was in school. Also, over half of his school was attended in Texas, which many believe to be about ten years behind the social digression of schools in California. Lastly, he receives calls daily from parents, teachers, and students who are dealing with *major problems* in their public schools, as evidenced by some of the cases we mentioned previously. As these calls grow more frequent, Brad's frustration and concern over public schooling has greatly increased.

SCHOOLING OPTIONS

In view of the rapid serious changes taking place in public schools, parents are strongly encouraged to consider *all* of the educational options for their children, including private schooling, charter schools, public school independent study, tutoring, and home schooling (which is also considered private schooling in some states). Considering these options does not imply that it is time for you to give up on your public school. *However, many schools have crossed the line by insisting on teaching revisionist history, pushing the homosexual agenda, and compromising educational standards.* Recent state legislation will only accelerate this trend. If your school has crossed that line and you consequently are no longer willing to send your children there, we commend you. For such parents, we have included a brief description of some of these viable educational options.

Private Schools

All private schools may seem very similar, but they are actually quite different. Even private schools that hold themselves out to be Christian or religious have at times shocked parents who have NOT CAREFULLY reviewed the practices of the private school. For example, one private parochial school in Northern California reportedly passed out Playboy and Playgirl magazines to a class of seventh graders without prior notice. Unlike public schools, egregious acts by private schools are generally unable to be litigated, leaving only one option, to remove your child. That case is a rarity, and there are still many good private schools in the country. We just ask that you not enroll them in a private school, wave good-bye, and figure everything will turn out fine. The bottom line: Private schools need to be carefully checked out before you enroll your child in one.

Home Schooling or Private Tutoring

Of all educational options, home schooling has become the fastest growing and, overall, has the highest academic success. This option should be given serious consideration. Some parents home school on their own choosing from a plethora of educational resources. Others prefer to home school through a consortium of home school families, sometimes organized through their local church. Check with your church to find out what programs they may have for home schooling families. You may be surprised at what you find. Most of my family attends Adventure Christian Church in Roseville, California. Brad and I usually attend one of their Saturday night services and, while there, we once noticed a brochure detailing their ministry to those who home school. Because we are considering this option, we were excited to see the opportunities available to us.

Home schooling is understandably becoming a viable option because it allows parents complete control over what their child is learning. There are also plenty of social and elective venues available for home schooled children. For example, in a consortium, there are often competitions like speech and debate, which can even go national through various national home school organizations. There are also athletic opportunities through private and some public schools. The opportunities are endless, and if you are unhappy with your particular school district, home schooling is a rising option to consider.

Charter Schools

Charter schooling is also becoming more common as more and more parents become unhappy with our public school system. Although a charter school is generally free from the state mandates and regulations, the charter school is still categorized as a public school and receives public funding. Parents need to examine the charter school to see that it meets their standard of expectation. Some are completely secular and possibly very liberal in their academic and social philosophy. Others may be very parent centered. It is not uncommon for such charter schools to be partially headed by clergy and use church facilities.

Public School Independent Study

Most school districts offer independent study programs where the child is still enrolled at the public school, but the child does their schooling at home. The school sometimes allows alternative educational resources and textbooks. However, they often provide textbooks and require that they be used. Depending on their position and level of control, this option is often, at least partially, self-defeating. Nonetheless, parents desiring their children to participate in public school athletics or other extracurricular activities may wish to consider this.

Finally, please remember that although the leadership of the Pacific Justice Institute has its personal preferences, the organization is committed to defending the rights of *parents* to decide what *they* think is best for their children.

Children—Our Responsibility

To sum up, children are a gift from God, and the responsibility for raising them falls on the parents. In this day and age of immorality and questionable ethics, parenting is not an easy job. Those who choose to compromise rather than commit to being a responsible and loving parent are inadvertently choosing to allow their children to be bombarded with harmful material. Parents will often demean other parents who decide to take a stand for decency and morality. Today there is a lot of pressure to be your children's "friends," rather than parent them and hold them accountable. As a youth minister, I have encountered a number of parents who did not want to "bother" their kids by parenting too much. In fact, one of my greatest hindrances in implementing effective ministry was the parents themselves. Unfortunately, I am talking about both non-Christian and Christian parents who had the mindset that being their kids' friends was more important than setting them straight. I have seen the result of that type of parenting, and it is not a good one. Proverbs 22:6 says, *"Train a child in the way he should go, and when he is old he will not turn from it."* I realize this promise from Proverbs sounds very simple, but it is God's Word; therefore, it is truth.

It is time that parents take a stand for the sake of their children. This means making decisions that are in the best interest of the children regardless of what they or others think. It also means protecting them in every facet of life including school. Finally, taking a stand for the children includes taking advantage of the evangelism opportunities God has provided for us in public schools. Training our children can best be summed up by a passage in the book of Deuteronomy:

> *"Love the Lord your God with all your heart and with all your soul and with all your strength. These commandments that I give you today are to be upon your hearts. Impress them on your children. Talk about them when you sit at home and when you walk along the road, when you lie down and when you get up. Tie them as symbols on your hands and bind them on your foreheads. Write them on the doorframes of your houses and on your gates."*[56]

7

WHAT'S A SCHOOL TO DO?
Suggested School Board Policies

Discrimination in the Name of Fairness?

A parent in a Northern California school district contacted our office. She informed me that the school board was meeting to vote on a policy regarding "discriminatory harassment" and that she had some reservations about who was attending this meeting to put forth their suggested policy. Instead of simply accepting the "inevitable", she took action to find out what this policy contained. She found out that the ACLU (American Civil Liberties Union) was suggesting a policy that was limited to giving special rights to homosexual students only. The Pacific Justice Institute drafted another policy that did not give special rights to one group of students. Rather, it gave the same rights to all students to be free from harassment, whether it was for their looks, their religion, their race, or *any other reason*. The ACLU was surprised, to say the least, when this policy was proposed at the school board meeting by one of our attorneys. Imagine their amazement when the school board voted to accept *this **inclusive** policy, drafted by PJI, rather than the **exclusive** one drafted by the ACLU. This change was made because one person stood up for what was right and what would be most helpful to students.

Proposed School Board Policies

The Pacific Justice Institute has written a variety of suggested school board policies. These policies cover various subjects and will be helpful to your local school board as they attempt to draft policies that are fair for all students and parents. If you have a favorable relationship with your principal, you may want to give him or her a set of these policies and ask him or her to speak to the school board. In this section we have included a summary of proposed policies. If you have any questions regarding any of these policies, please contact us.

It should be noted that these policies may be subject to statutory limitations in your state.

PROPOSED SCHOOL BOARD POLICY #1
Absenteeism

Any student absent due to illness shall not be required to serve a make-up day if the student has a signed letter from a medical health practitioner or parent validating the illness. However, the student will not be exempt from making up the work required in the class.

PROPOSED SCHOOL BOARD POLICY #2
Apologies

A public school parent or guardian is entitled to an apology when a teacher, staff, or administrator makes an obvious mistake in judgment or violates school district policy, which affects that parent or guardian's child. Likewise, the child is entitled to an apology when that mistake has directly and adversely impacted that child.

PROPOSED SCHOOL BOARD POLICY #3
Equal Access

During non-school hours, use of school facilities shall be made equally available to all community groups.

PROPOSED SCHOOL BOARD POLICY #4
Corporal Punishment

Absent a reasonable suspicion of abuse or neglect by parents, school personnel shall respect the rights of parents choosing to use corporal punishment, without the school retaliating.

PROPOSED SCHOOL BOARD POLICY #5
Evolution

"Because 'nothing in science or in any other field of knowledge shall be taught dogmatically' and 'scientific theories are constantly subject to testing, modification, and refutation as new evidence and new ideas emerge,' teachers in this school district are expected to help students analyze scientific strengths and weaknesses of existing scientific theories, including the theory of evolution." [57]

PROPOSED SCHOOL BOARD POLICY #6
Films

"R", "NC-17", or other adult-rated films will not be shown to students on school grounds. "PG 13" films may not be shown without written consent from parent or guardian. Any films with a "PG" rating or those that have not been rated by the Motion Picture Association of America (MPAA) shall not be shown without prior approval of the Book Review Committee or prior written consent from parent or guardian. Parental written consent forms must include the film's MPAA rating. The teacher desiring to show the film must preview the film to ensure that it is age appropriate and has direct relationship to the curriculum.

PROPOSED SCHOOL BOARD POLICY #7
Graduation Message

The following is an example of graduation speech policy that was found to be constitutional by the 11th Circuit.

1. The use of a brief opening and/or closing message, not to exceed two minutes, at high school graduation exercises shall rest within the discretion of the graduation senior class;
2. The opening and/or closing message shall be given by a student volunteer, a member of the graduating class, chosen by the graduating senior class as a whole;
3. If the graduating senior class chooses to use an opening and/or closing message, the content of that message shall be prepared by the student volunteer and shall not be monitored or otherwise reviewed by the County School Board, its officers or employees.

The US Supreme Court refused to hear the appeal, essentially affirming the constitutionality of the above policy. [58] The purpose of these guidelines is to allow students to direct their own graduation message without monitoring or review by school officials.

PROPOSED SCHOOL BOARD POLICY #8
Harassment—Discriminatory

Discriminatory harassment is any verbal, visual, or physical conduct, which is sufficiently severe, persistent, or pervasive so that it adversely affects, or has the purpose or logical consequence of interfering with the student's educational program or creates an intimidating, hostile, or offensive school atmosphere. Harassment, whether it is by students, staff, or third parties in the school community, is strictly prohibited, and will subject the perpetrator to disciplinary action. Harassment, regardless of its basis, is prohibited.

PROPOSED SCHOOL BOARD POLICY #9
School Book/Film Selection

With the exception of health and science books, no books or films containing pornography, drawings or photography containing nudity (exception for classical works), or explicit descriptions of sexual activities will be allowed in the public school libraries or classrooms.

All books or films being considered for use by a teacher or for placement in a school library will first require the majority of approval of a Book Review Committee (BRC). The BRC will be composed of nine parents of children enrolled in the school district. The BRC parents shall be chosen by the school board and shall not be employed by the district.

PROPOSED SCHOOL BOARD POLICY #10
Opt-Out Forms

At the beginning of every school year, the school district shall provide parents and guardians with an opt-out form that will allow a parent or guardian to excuse their children from any instruction, discussions, films, etc. that violate the religious or moral convictions of the parents or guardians.

PROPOSED SCHOOL BOARD POLICY #11
Parental Consent

In sensitivity to the diverse cultural and religious beliefs and values of the parents and families in the community, no instruction or supervised discussions involving the topic of sex or sexual orientation shall commence at any time without the prior written consent of a pupil's parent or guardian.

PROPOSED SCHOOL BOARD POLICY #12
Pledge of Allegiance

At the beginning of each school day, the teacher shall lead the students in the Pledge of Allegiance. Teachers are not allowed to lead the students in any other pledge other than the Pledge of Allegiance, which should be said in its entirety, without removal of any part.

PROPOSED SCHOOL BOARD POLICY #13
Political Viewpoints

All academic instructors are forbidden from expressing either verbally or silently their personal viewpoints on controversial or political matters during classroom instructional time. Any class discussions regarding political or social issues must be moderated by the instructor in a neutral manner.

PROPOSED SCHOOL BOARD POLICY #14
Prior Notice for Instruction

Prior notice shall be provided to all parents or guardians regarding any instruction, whether in the classroom or in an assembly, involving issues of sexual controversy, such as sexual orientation.

PROPOSED SCHOOL BOARD POLICY #15
Programs and Presentations

Any school program or presentation addressing controversial moral, religious, sexual, political, or social issues must be presented in a balanced manner which ensures the presentation of alternative views.

PROPOSED SCHOOL BOARD POLICY #16
Religious Instruction

Religious instruction, which may be included in history, English, elective classes, etc., or acknowledgement of religious holidays, must be conducted in a non-proselytizing manner.

PROPOSED SCHOOL BOARD POLICY #17
Renting of Facilities

A religious institution (e.g. church, synagogue, etc.) may lease a public school facility on a regular basis during the weekend for a period of up to five years. At the end of such time, the religious institution may renew their lease on an annual basis if there is not another religious institution(s) that has applied and is eligible for usage of the same facility for the same time of day. However, in order to receive usage preference, the completed lease application by other religious institutions must be received and approved by the District at least three months prior to the expiration of the existing lease. Preference between such applicants shall be granted based upon which completed application was first received by the District.

The District shall not deny, limit, or encumber a religious institution's usage of school facilities based upon the religious beliefs, practices, or denominational or sectarian affiliation of that religious institution. A religious institution denied usage of a public school facility will, upon request, be provided a written explanation as to all reasons for the denial. The rental rate charged to a religious institution shall not exceed the actual direct costs to the school district resulting from the religious institution's leasing the school facility.

PROPOSED SCHOOL BOARD POLICY #18
Reprimands

Students will not be reprimanded or demeaned for statements, positions, or actions by the student, parent, or guardian in conflict with a teacher's personal views on political or social policies or issues. To demean includes the teacher conveying to other students that the student's belief is out of step, extreme, or any other word that places the student's views in a negative light.

PROPOSED SCHOOL BOARD POLICY #19
Report Cards

Any club in which a student has attended two or more times shall be listed on the student's report card. The leadership position will also be included. A failure to report a student's participation in a club may result in the student's failure to gain admittance to a particular college or university. A failure to report a student's participation in a club may result in the need for a change in club sponsors.

PROPOSED SCHOOL BOARD POLICY #20
Solemn Expression before School Board Meetings

The school board shall begin their meetings with a moment of solemn expression. Any member of the community who is the first to sign up shall deliver the solemn expression. The purpose of a solemn expression before public meetings is to assist school board members in remembering the seriousness of their oaths and obligations as elected public servants.

PROPOSED SCHOOL BOARD POLICY #21
Solemn Expression before Athletic Events

School District sponsored athletic events shall commence with a moment of solemn expression by a student or a parent of a student attending the event. The first to sign up to deliver the solemn expression shall be selected for the event. The purpose of this moment of solemn expression is to help promote positive sportsmanship among the participants.

PROPOSED SCHOOL BOARD POLICY #22
Requests Regarding Teachers

Public school parents have the right to have their child removed from the classroom of a teacher who the parents believe cannot adequately teach their child. Parents have the right to request placement of their child in a particular teacher's classroom, and expect that the principal will make such accommodation when at all possible. Likewise, parents are entitled to know the specific reasons why such accommodation cannot be made and are allowed to appeal the decision to the superintendent.

PROPOSED SCHOOL BOARD POLICY #23
School Presentations

School presentations and field trips which are political and/or controversial in nature shall be approved in advance by the Superintendent and/or his or her designee as well as by the student's parent(s) and/or guardian(s) prior to students being allowed to participate in the activity.

PROPOSED SCHOOL BOARD POLICY #24
Teacher Communication

The right of a parent or guardian to speak directly with his or her child's teacher shall not be abridged or removed except for risks of bona fide health or safety concerns. It is also the right of a parent to expect that a teacher return a parent's call, e-mail, or note within seventy-two hours. The School District shall encourage frequent and positive communication between parents and classroom teachers regarding the academic and social development of students.

PROPOSED SCHOOL BOARD POLICY # 25
Teachers' Right to Notify Parents

A public school teacher is free to give students' parents or guardians prior accurate notice regarding any instruction, presentation, material, activity, or class discussion about which the teacher reasonably feels any of the students' parents may wish to be notified.

PROPOSED SCHOOL BOARD POLICY #26
Union Dues

All school district employees shall be provided written notice of their right to have all of their union dues diverted to a mutually agreeable 501(c)(3) charity, as per Federal law, upon a proper showing to the union of the employee's sincere, deep convictions or religiously based objection to paying such dues.[59] This notice shall also be posted in a place at the school commonly accessible to school faculty (e.g., teacher's lounge). In addition, district employees shall be provided written notice of their right to have a deduction in their union dues, based upon political objector status as per Federal law.

PROPOSED SCHOOL BOARD POLICY #27
Instruction
Family Life/Sex Education

In all sex education courses that discuss sexual intercourse, course material and instruction shall:

1. Be age appropriate.

2. Stress that abstinence is the only contraceptive method which is 100% effective, and that all other methods of contraception carry a risk of failure in preventing unwanted pregnancy. Statistics based on the latest medical information shall be provided to students citing the failure and success rate of condoms and other contraceptives in preventing pregnancy.

3. Stress that sexually transmitted diseases are serious possible hazards of sexual intercourse. Students shall be provided the failure and success rates of condoms in preventing AIDS and other sexually transmitted diseases.

4. Include a discussion of the possible emotional and psychological consequences of preadolescent and adolescent sexual intercourse outside of marriage and the consequences of unwanted adolescent pregnancy.

5. Stress that students should abstain from sexual intercourse until marriage.

6. Teach honor and respect for monogamous heterosexual marriage.

7. Advise students of the laws pertaining to their financial responsibility to children born in and out of wedlock.

8. Advise students that it is unlawful for males of any age to have sexual relations with females

under the age of 18 to whom they are not married pursuant to state law (e.g., California Penal Code 6215).

9. Emphasize that the student has the power to control personal behavior. Students shall be encouraged to base their actions on reasoning, self-discipline, sense of responsibility, self-control, and ethical considerations such as respect for one's self and others.

10. Teach students to not make unwanted physical and verbal sexual advances and how to say no to unwanted sexual advances. Students shall be taught that it is wrong to take advantage of, or to exploit, another person. The material and instruction shall also encourage youth to resist negative peer pressure.

PROPOSED SCHOOL BOARD POLICY #28
Students Leaving Campus

With the exception of medical emergencies, no student shall be dismissed from campus during school hours without the written consent of a parent or guardian. In case of medical emergencies, parents or guardians shall be contacted as soon as possible as to where their child was taken for medical care.

8

WHAT IF I DON'T REMEMBER?
Practical Ways to Share the Gospel

*"Therefore go and make disciples of all nations, baptizing
them in the name of the Father and of the Son and of the Holy Spirit,
and teaching them to obey everything I have commanded you."*
Matthew 28:19-20a (NIV)

As stated in the previous chapters, the Bible commands all believers
to tell others about Jesus, His death on the cross, and His resurrection. Not everyone is called to preach from street corners or approach
strangers, but we are still called to look for opportunities, and as the
Lord leads, to share our faith.

Evangelism or sharing the Gospel should be viewed as a process,
not a program. You can learn and use different evangelism programs
like the Four Spiritual Laws or the Roman Path (Road), which we will
be discussing in this chapter. These programs are good and helpful.
However, evangelism is much more than learning and sharing a four-step salvation plan. In this chapter we will talk about three different
aspects of evangelism. First, we will talk about lifestyle evangelism and
how our lifestyle and actions are a testimony to our faith in Christ. Second, we will discuss how to share the truth of the Gospel and in what
ways we should be prepared to show someone how to accept Christ.
Third, we will discuss friendship evangelism and why our first mission
field is our sphere of influence.

Lifestyle Evangelism

"You may be the only Bible people ever read." This well-known
saying indicates that when we simply live as Christians, we share our
faith. This is often called lifestyle evangelism. ***People will observe your
Christian faith before they will ask you about it.*** At school, for example, as word gets around that you are a Christian, students will begin to
watch you to see what that means. Sound a little intimidating? Don't

worry; you do not have to be perfect. Being a good Christian does not mean being a perfect person. Rather, being a good Christian means humbly asking God to guide you in every situation of your life. It also means listening to the still, small voice of the Holy Spirit telling you when you ought not to say something . . . or when you should. Here are some examples of what it means to evangelize by your lifestyle.

Respond and react in a way that gives glory and honor to God

When you respond and react to situations at school—whether as a student, teacher, administrator, or parent—people will watch you to see if you act as a Christian ought to. Essentially they will observe you to see if you act differently than your peers who have no religious foundation. When you do react differently than those who have no moral base, it may open the door for them to ask you about your faith. When you do not respond in anger or with swearing, or when you do not laugh at dirty jokes and refuse to put up with gossip, people will notice that and quite possibly ask you about it. (This also works at home, work, the gym, or in any other social situation.) When things happen in your life, both good and bad, people will notice how you react to those situations also. We do not mean to imply that you should be so composed, stoic, and nonchalant that nothing phases you. We all have emotions, and it is not wrong to be ecstatic when something good happens and sorrowful when something bad happens. However, when something good happens, we can give the glory to God. As it says in the book of James, *"Every good and perfect gift is from above, coming down from the Father of the heavenly lights, who does not change like shifting shadows."*[60] God deserves the glory, and it should be given to Him. Likewise, when something difficult is happening in your life, you can have sadness; however, you ought not be despondent to the point of giving up altogether because all hope is lost. No, we have a living hope and trust in God, the creator of heaven and earth. And even when you do not understand something in your life, you still, in faith, can trust in God and His Word. As a Christian you know that doing so will help you through difficult trials.

A benefit to being a Christian is the provision God has given via the church body and pastors. You are not alone as you journey through good times and bad. Not only do you have God, who says He will never leave you nor forsake you, God also provides the church and pastors to help Christians, including you, through tough times. Do not take the church for granted. God purposefully and providentially placed you in a church body for you to learn, grow, and be encouraged. His word says to *"not give up meeting together as some are in the habit of doing, but let us encourage one another . . ."*[61] Involvement in the church is essential to living the life God has called you to, thereby enabling you to share your faith through your lifestyle.

Your lifestyle can open many doors to sharing your faith. Keep your eyes open for opportunities to evangelize through the life that you live. You will find that people will ask you to pray for them or give them advice in certain situations because they respect that you have an absolute belief and are not wavering in that belief. *Lifestyle evangelism is an exciting way to share your faith!*

Share personal stories and testimonies of God's work in your life

As I mentioned before, one of Brad's favorite subjects to talk about with strangers was our pledge of sexual abstinence before marriage. While at a swap meet in Orange County, Brad decided to share our pledge with a couple of mattress salesmen, both of whom were in their late twenties or early thirties. It is always interesting to see how people react to our story. Both salespeople, one man and one woman, listened intently. Then the young man, with a contemplative and sorrowful look, said, "I wish I'd done that." This man was not a believer, nor did he subscribe to any religious foundation at all. Yet he still regretted what he had done and, for a reason unknown to him, he knew what we had done was best. As friends, fellow students, and teachers observe you living your life quite differently than the rest of the world, questions will inevitably follow. Whether you are a student, teacher, or parent, you may have a story like ours that includes abstaining from sex until marriage. Your personal story may include why and how you are able to say no to drugs and drinking, or how Jesus set you free from past bondage of sin. Or maybe your story is how, by God's faithfulness and promise of peace, you are able to trust Him in the midst of a family death, disease, or tragedy of some kind. The questions and answers that come from sharing your stories can easily move into a discussion of spiritual matters, which will eventually lead you to sharing your life-changing decision to follow Christ.

None of us have any idea what may touch the heart of an unbeliever. Don't underestimate God and what He is leading you to share. Each of us has had our own evangelism experience. What touched one of us may not have touched another. Many of us have experienced messages from ministers and missionaries that God has used as a tool to grasp the heart of an unbeliever. I have witnessed people responding to a message while I have stood there wondering why that particular message was so compelling. God has used the beauty of creation, the artistry of videos and music, and unpredictable changes or trials in people's lives to bring them to His throne.

One time when Brad was speaking at a church, the Holy Spirit kept prompting him to share something specific about a serious auto accident he had when he was a teenager. He kept pushing the thought away because he was trying to keep on track with his sermon. Finally, realizing this was something God really wanted said, he paused, told the congregation what was happening, and then shared what God put on his heart. Afterwards, a woman approached him and told him that what he shared in those moments was exactly what she was experiencing and what she needed to hear at that time. Brad and I have both experienced times of speaking to groups where God has continually put something on our hearts to share that we had not planned. When we obey God's leading, He often shows us afterwards why He wanted us to share that specific story, scripture, or experience. Be sensitive to God and what He is leading you to share with others.

Sharing the Truth of the Gospel

Lifestyle evangelism is important, but it is not enough if it doesn't eventually lead us to share the truth of the Gospel with another. Therefore, we need to be ready and willing to share the truth when asked and give a reason for the hope we have in the Lord. Paul writes in Romans, "How, then, can they call on the one they have not believed in? And how can they believe in the one of whom they have not heard? **And how can they hear without someone preaching to them?**"[62]

Brad works out at the gym about three times a week. When we first got married, I was confused about why he often stayed at the gym so long when he went. He would leave for the gym, which is just down the street, and sometimes return home a couple of hours later. I understood that he wanted a good workout, but I wondered what could take three hours. Then one evening I understood what he was doing. He came home excited about the sharing he had done with someone at the gym. This individual was living a homosexual life, but was interested in hearing about how much Brad loved marriage and how incredible it was to be a Christian and walk with the Lord. By the end of the conversation, this young man agreed to visit our church where they have a ministry to homosexuals. With his permission, Brad called the pastor in charge of this ministry and gave him this man's name and phone number. I realized then that Brad often took so long at the gym, and other places, because he loved to share the Lord with everyone he met, even strangers. It continually amazes me how good Brad is at starting up conversations with strangers in lines, at stores, almost anywhere. You may be one of those who is comfortable talking with strangers and people you meet every day. If so, that is great! But even if you are not comfortable, God is calling you to share with someone and each one of us ought to be ready to do so. We can share the Gospel in so many ways, and sharing with strangers is just one option.

THE ROMAN PATH

There are many different methods or strategies by which to remember the Gospel according to Scriptures. For the purpose of brevity, I am going to share my personal favorite. I went to a private Christian High School called Village Christian, in Sun Valley, California. One of my high school Bible classes (taught by Bo Boshers) had probably the greatest impact on my life. That class was very practical and applicable to the daily life of a Christian. I will never forget how our teacher literally forced us to memorize, and get tested on, numerous times, what is often called the Roman Path (Some people know it as the Roman Road). I say that he forced us because if my memory serves me right, the other option was failing the class. Over my years in youth ministry I have heard a variety of verse configurations that is termed the Roman Path. There is not one that is more right than another. I will simply be sharing the one that was taught to me and has stuck with me for over sixteen years. Because I memorized the Roman Path in the New International Version, I used the same version for this book. For your benefit use the version of the Bible that is most familiar to you. This list of verses gives a clear scriptural progression of how to bring one to belief in Christ. It is the truth of the Gospel, which God's Word makes clear.

The Roman Path begins with **Romans 3:23** which says, *"For all have sinned and fall short of the glory of God."* What does that mean? It means that we have "missed the mark." It means that none of us is perfect, and we cannot reach God without some help.

Romans 6:23 shows us that there are consequences for our sin. It says, *"For the wages of sin is death but the gift of God is eternal life in Christ Jesus our Lord."* This verse informs us of the consequences of our sin, then quickly assures us that there is an answer to our struggle with sin, which is found in Jesus Christ.

Romans 5:8-9 further explains this gift and makes clear to us God's awesome love. *"But God demonstrates his own love for us in this: While we were still sinners, Christ died for us. Since we have now been justified by his blood, how much more shall we be saved from God's wrath through Him!"*

Romans 10:13, 9-10 begins with a wonderful promise and then tells us what we ought to do next. *"For everyone who calls on the name of the Lord will be saved. That if you confess with your mouth, 'Jesus is Lord,' and believe in your heart that God raised him from the dead, you will be saved. For it is with your heart that you believe and are justified, and it is with your mouth that you confess and are saved."* After explaining what we ought to do, God's Word then gives us an exciting promise.

This promise is found in **Romans 8:1**. That verse says, *"Therefore, there is now no condemnation for those who are in Christ Jesus."* How amazing God's love is that despite all we do wrong, we are still found righteous because of Christ's death on the cross and our acceptance of that love.

Finally, the last two verses from the Roman Path that I learned long ago are not from Romans at all. Don't worry, this is not intentionally meant to confuse you. Two of the most important concepts for Christians to grasp are the forgiveness of sins and the assurance of salvation. **1 John 1:9** says, *"If we confess our sins, He is faithful and just and will forgive us our sins and purify us from all unrighteousness."* This is a promise from God that He will forgive us our sins if we sincerely confess them to Him.

The last verse answers that question I heard so many times in my years of youth ministry: "How can I **know** I am saved?" I always turn to *1 John 5:11-13*, which says, *"And this is the testimony: God has given us eternal life, and this life is in his Son. He who has the Son has life; he who does not have the Son of God does not have life. I write these things to you who believe in the name of the Son of God so that you may know that you have eternal life."*

This is one of the most exciting and fulfilling passages in the Bible. I remember learning this verse and understanding its meaning when I was just a high school student. As I began to understand the importance of this passage, a peace washed over me, and I realized I never needed to doubt my salvation in the Lord.

As stated previously, other versions of the Roman Path exist and one is not better than another. The example above is simply the one I learned. Memorizing this long ago gave me the assurance that anywhere, at anytime, I could walk someone through the gospel message by using the Bible. I remember one time my memorization was put to the test. One of my assignments in Bible College was to go to a men's homeless shelter and preach a sermon to them before they could eat. The instructions were simple. I needed to share a Biblical sermon and speak for *at least* twenty minutes. The people in charge were very insistent that the message could *not* be shorter than twenty minutes. I had never done this before, and was a little nervous. I don't remember the message I shared, but I do remember being done with it in just over ten minutes. Most people speak too fast when they are nervous, and that is exactly what I did. Therefore, a twenty-minute message turned into ten. Standing at the makeshift pulpit in a homeless shelter with approximately fifty men staring at me, I quickly shared the first thing that came to my mind. I dove into the Roman Path and shared each verse and its meaning. The second part of the message went rather well, and I was pleased that I had memorized the Roman Path because I was able to share the simple, saving truth of the gospel. For easy reading and memorization, I have listed the scripture references and an easy paraphrase of each of the verses:

Romans 3:23	=>	All have sinned.
Romans 6:23	=>	The cost of that sin is death.
Romans 5:8-9	=>	Christ paid the penalty. He died for us.
Romans 10:13, 9-10	=>	Confess that Jeus is Lord and believe in Him.
Romans 8:1	=>	If we accept the Lord, we are no longer condemned.
1 John 1:9	=>	God forgives our sins.
1 John 5:11-13	=>	We have eternal life in the Lord.

Some people are intimidated about memorizing the Roman Path for fear that when the time comes, they will forget one or more of the verses. Don't worry. In my Bible class, I was also taught an easy, ten-step process to remember this path. It requires that you memorize only one scripture reference (not even the whole verse!), and you have to keep your Bible handy. The reference you will need to memorize is Romans 3:23. If you remember that one reference, you are home free. Write it on a piece of paper and stick it on your bathroom mirror. Put it on the dashboard of your car or where you will see it every day, usually more than once. While you are reading this book, grab your Bible if possible and walk through each of these easy steps.

STEP #1 - Look up Romans 3:23. Remember that is the only reference you have to memorize in order to get started.

STEP #2 - Now that you have memorized that reference and looked it up, take a pen and write the next reference, Romans 6:23 on the bottom of the page that has Romans 3:23 on it.

STEP #3 - Now turn to Romans 6:23.

STEP #4 - On the bottom of that page, write the next verse, Romans 5:8-9 on the bottom of that page.

STEP #5 - Now turn to Romans 5:8-9.

STEP #6 - On the bottom of that page, write Romans 10:13, 9-10.

STEP #7 - Now turn to Romans 10:13, 9-10.

STEP #8 - On the bottom of that page, write Romans 8:1.

STEP #9 - Now turn to Romans 8:1.

STEP #10 - On the bottom of that page, write 1 John 1:9.

STEP #11 - Now turn to 1 John 1:9.

STEP #12 - On the bottom of that page, write 1 John 5:11-13.

As you can see, in order to remember the Roman Path all you need to do is remember–**Romans 3:23**. If you can remember Romans 3:23 and can look that up in your Bible, the verses you have written on the bottom of that page will lead you to the next verse, and so on and so on, until you have reached the end. Hopefully the explanation of the Roman Path is as helpful to you as it was for me. If not, do not get discouraged. Remember that this is just one of many ways to remember the Gospel. I simply shared the one that worked best for me. The most important thing is for you to choose the way that works for you. For Brad, the four spiritual laws booklet was most helpful for him. You can pick up a booklet that explains the four spiritual laws at your church or local Christian bookstore.

Again, there are *many* ways to share the Gospel. What is essential is that you share it. God may surprise you. He does that, you know. The person you thought least likely to come to the Lord is often the one who is most responsive to you.

The Story of Roger and Doug

Take Roger, for example. Roger was a popular student and athlete in high school. He seemed to have it all together. One day as he was driving home from school he saw a fellow student named Doug walking down the street. They were not in the same "crowd" at school, so they did not really know each other. For some reason, Roger pulled over and asked Doug if he wanted a ride home. Doug gratefully accepted, and a valuable friendship began. They were from different sides of the world, both literally and figuratively. Roger grew up in their community while Doug grew up in another country, doing ministry work with his parents. Roger had always been in the popular crowd at school with lots of friends, and he was involved in athletics and school activities. Doug was not unpopular; he was simply an average student, studying hard, and developing just a couple of strong friendships. Doug often talked to Roger about his relationship with God. Even though Roger was popular and confident, Doug was not swayed or intimidated by that. Over time, Roger began asking Doug questions about God and church, and eventually he accepted an invitation to a church event. As time passed, Roger admitted to Doug that he needed God in his life. Doug shared with him how to ask God into his life and what it meant to live for Him. Many years have passed since that time, and now both Roger and Doug are in the vocational ministry and walking closely with the Lord. Doug could have looked at this popular student and not taken the time to share the Lord with him. Instead, he listened to God's prompting on his heart. God is using these two men today to change hundreds of lives for the Kingdom because Doug listened and took action.

Trusting God

If we listen to God and obey Him, He will take us to places we never thought possible. Also, if we listen to God's prompting like Doug did and share with our fellow student or teacher, we may be surprised to see that person embrace God's love, whether it happens immediately or over a period of time as a friendship is developed. The key is not to become discouraged when we share the Gospel, regardless of the results. *Discouragement is damaging, and it is not the place wherein God wants us to dwell.* **He wants us to dwell on His power and His presence and His peace in our lives.** In my experience, there have been many times when the person I was sharing with simply listened, thanked me for sharing, and went on with his or her life. When I first began sharing my faith, I would feel badly or think I had failed in some way. In short, I would take the rejection personally. It is true that we like to see immediate results even though developing a friendship may be what is needed first. If we are so concerned about being rejected, we will not take the time to develop a deep friendship that may be very constructive in that person's accepting the Lord.

It is important to remember that God is in control. It is He who draws people to Him, and those people have a free will to accept or not accept His love and calling. Even though the person you share with may not ask to accept Christ right then and there, you are "planting seeds" in his or her life. After you have planted the seeds, pray for that person, and then allow God and the Holy Spirit to work on that person's heart.

Friendship Evangelism

The Greek word for household is oikos. It means: *your sphere of influence.* Every person has a unique *oikos* or sphere of influence. In fact, there are no two alike. Students, think about the different classes you are in; and teachers, think about the different classes you teach. Each one is unique. Your mission field is that sphere—family, friends, people at work, school, etc. Sharing your faith with your friends at school, or your fellow teachers, or your children's teacher is where God has put you right now. Honor Him by beginning to pray for people in your sphere of influence. Then begin to share as God leads you to do so both by your lifestyle and by directly sharing the gospel. For students, the youth ministry department at Saddleback Community Church in Mission Viejo, California, has put together a simple five-step process to make it easy for you to reach out to your friends.

#1 – Tell your friend that you are a Christian.

#2 – Invite your friend to an appropriate program at church.

#3 – Tell your friend why you are a Christian.

#4 – Tell your friend how you became a Christian.

#5 – Ask your friend if he or she would like to become a Christian.

This five-step process to reach out to your friends may sound incredibly simple. It is! We encourage you to pick your first friend and start your friendship evangelism right away. We are confident that doing this will transform both his or her life and yours!

9

WHAT'S YOUR STORY?
The Three Parts of Sharing Your Testimony

"A good testimony is one that does not glorify the past but glorifies what God is doing in your life in the present."
—Greg Laurie

What is a Testimony?

You have probably heard this word bantered about in church or religious circles. If you are not familiar with the word in its religious usage, it may be familiar to you in terms of a courtroom and a witness giving testimony for a trial. I have always enjoyed watching shows and movies and reading books about trials and court cases. I never imagined I would actually marry an attorney; watching these shows is of even more interest now. When Brad and I watch the television series *Law and Order*, he enjoys guessing which way the criminal case and then the trial will turn out. I remember one episode in which a witness for the prosecution not only had a story to tell, but was eager to tell it. This witness enthusiastically offered information about the defendant and about the crime for which he had been charged. It may sound strange, but a Christian essentially does the same thing. Christians, when sharing their testimony, tell why they came to Christ, how they came to know and believe in Him, and how their lives have changed because of Him. These are the three parts of a testimony.

Telling Your Story

Everyone can share about his or her life *before* Christ. Some people have a radical testimony of drugs and bad living. Some have grown up in the church and gradually came to realize they too were sinners and had to make the choice to accept or reject Christ as their Lord and Savior. Still others may have been nice people who lived a relatively good life, who realized they needed to fill a void in their life. Maybe one or none of these scenarios sounds familiar to you. Whatever the story, each one is unique and each one was written as a testimony to the grace and forgiveness of God.

Maybe you cannot fully understand and explain how God touched you and brought you to Him. It may be something that is inexplicable, yet powerful and that's just fine. Paul spoke of God's inexplicable grace in Scripture—so amazing, it is hard to understand. One day, God spoke to you and you obeyed. You cannot explain it nor do you try. Only those who have experienced the same can understand it. And even they cannot explain it nor totally understand it. Again, it is okay not to understand God and all His ways. One of my professors once said, and I never forgot it, "If we understood God, He would cease to be God." In other words, why don't we understand everything about God? Simply because He is God. Why should we expect to understand everything about the Creator of the universe and all that exists? We cannot explain everything about Him, and we cannot explain exactly how He drew us to Him. But He did, and that is the important part.

Be wary of those who say, "I have been a Christian *all my life,*" or "I was *born that way.*" Being born to Christian parents does not automatically make you Christian. Individuals are still responsible for the decisions they make, and one of those decisions is whether or not they choose to live for the Lord. While I worked with youth, I experienced numerous occasions when a student would tell me he or she had always been a Christian. I knew these young people often said this simply out of ignorance. It was true that they had been born into a Christian family and had always attended church, just as I had; but it was not necessarily true that they were walking with the Lord. Knowing this, I would explain to them that becoming a Christian is a personal decision. After I explained that at some point they had to come to the realization they were a sinner and needed the grace and forgiveness found only in the Lord, he or she would often realize they had done just that. They would recall a time, maybe at camp or at church, when they had made a concrete decision to follow the Lord and had been baptized in obedience to Him. If he or she realized they had never made such a decision, I encouraged them to make a decision that very day and also encouraged them to be baptized as a symbol of full obedience to God.

You may be like that young person who thought he had always been a Christian. It is valuable if you can pinpoint a time in your life when you accepted Christ, were baptized out of obedience to His Word, and made the choice to live for Him. I remember hearing a quote made by Dietrich Bonhoeffer, a follower of Christ, who was imprisoned and killed in Germany for his faith. Although I do not remember the source of this quote, I never forgot what he said. This is how Bonhoeffer describes our call to faith in the Lord.

> *"Alone you stood before God when He called you;*
> *alone you had to answer that call;*
> *alone you had to struggle and pray;*
> *and alone you will die and give an account to God.*
> *You cannot escape from yourself; for God has singled you out."*

Knowing when you became a follower of Christ is significant for you as a person and important if you want to evangelize in your school. An important part of sharing your faith is being able to share your testimony. This chapter will help you understand what a testimony is, and how you can write your own. Remember, it is valuable for you to try to pinpoint a time in which you came to walk in obedience to Christ by becoming a Christian. If you have not done that and would like to, please talk to your parents, your spouse, one of your pastors, or someone who is a dedicated follower of Christ. A mature Christian can help you rediscover the time you became a Christian or came to walk in obedience to Him.

Paul's Story

Whatever your background, whether it is dramatic in your opinion or not, your personal testimony will impact someone in some way. Testimonies are like fingerprints. No two are alike. God has spoken to each person in a unique and personal way. Your background does not matter. What matters is your decision to follow Christ. As I said before, there are three parts to a testimony:

• Who you were before Christ or *why you* came to Christ,

• *How* you came to Christ and,

• *How* your life has changed because of Christ.

Paul's testimony in Acts 22:1-21 is a perfect example of sharing one's testimony. It has the three parts I am talking about and gives the perfect example of how to share one's testimony. I used the New International Version of the Bible for this portion of the book also. While I know it is easy to skip or skim past Scripture in a book, please take the time to read the Scripture of Paul's testimony I've included. The verses you are about to read are Paul beginning to share his testimony. First, he shared who he was before Christ.

> *"Brothers and fathers, listen now to my defense. When they heard him speak to them in Aramaic, they became very quiet. Then Paul said, 'I am a Jew, born in Tarsus of Cilicia, but brought up in this city. Under Gamaliel I was thoroughly trained in the law of our fathers and was just as zealous for God as any of you are today. I persecuted the followers of this Way to their death, arresting both men and women and throwing them into prison, as also the high priest and all the Council can testify. I even obtained letters from them to their brothers in Damascus, and went there to bring these people as prisoners to Jerusalem to be punished.'" (Verses 1-5)*

In this first part, as Paul spoke before the leaders of that day, he shared what his life was like before he came to Christ. He shared that he was born a Jew and had knowledge and training about God and the law. He was angry and killing Christians because of their faith. He was a murderer! Paul's story is a perfect one for those of you who think you are not "good enough" to come to Christ.

During my youth ministry years, I met many young people who did not think they were good enough to come to Christ and live for Him. I explained to them that *that* was the point. They were *not* good enough, and they could *not* do enough to be forgiven. It was Christ who took on their sin when He was put to death on the cross. It was Christ who could save them, and nothing they did was too bad to be forgiven. Then I shared with them the story of Paul. I have found that young people really like to hear about Paul's testimony because it is a clear display of God's unending love regardless of what we do. All we have to do in response to His love is accept it. Once we accept that love and confess with our mouth that Jesus is Lord and believe it in our heart, we are saved. That is the exciting message of the gospel waiting to be shared with students, teachers, and adults in public schools everywhere!

As we continue reading Paul's testimony, we notice that Paul's story of his life *before* Christ is the shortest part of his testimony. He doesn't dwell on the past tragedies and glorify or put into detail the previous violence and anger in his life. He acknowledges it but quickly moves on to explain how Christ revealed Himself and how he came to believe in the Lord his Savior.

> *"About noon as I came near Damascus, suddenly a bright light from heaven flashed around me. I fell to the ground and heard a voice say to me, 'Saul, Saul! Why do you persecute me?'*
>
> *'Who are you Lord?' I asked.*
>
> *'I am Jesus of Nazareth, whom you are persecuting,' he replied. 'My companions saw the light but they did not understand the voice of him who was speaking to me.'*
>
> *'What shall I do Lord?' I asked.*
>
> *'Get up, the Lord said, and go into Damascus. There you will be told all that you have been assigned to do.' My companions led me by the hand into Damascus, because the brilliance of the light had blinded me'"*
> (Verses 6-11).

In verses six through eleven, Paul shares how Christ revealed Himself when he was traveling to Damascus. It was at that point that Paul, previously named Saul, realized he was not just persecuting Christians. He was also fighting against the Lord God Almighty. Knowing that he was no match, and witnessing the awesome presence and power of the Lord, Paul fell to his knees. Then the Lord sent Ananias to him to "bring him sight."

"A man named Ananias came to see me. He was a devout observer of the law and highly respected by all the Jews living there. He stood beside me and said, 'Brother Saul, receive your sight!' And at that very moment I was able to see him" (Verses 12-13).

While Ananias was sent by the Lord to open up Paul's eyes physically, it was even more important for Paul's eyes to be opened up spiritually. Before you and I met the Lord, we were in spiritual darkness, and we needed the light (Jesus) for our eyes to be opened.

Most of Paul's testimony covers how he came to Christ, and what happened after the fact. In verses fourteen through twenty-one, the Lord tells Paul specifically what he was to do in response to believing in Christ as Lord.

"Then he said: 'The God of our fathers has chosen you to know His will and to see the Righteous One and to hear words from His mouth. You will be His witness to all men of what you have seen and heard. And now what are you waiting for? Get up, be baptized and wash your sins away, calling on His name.'

When I returned to Jerusalem and was praying at the temple, I fell into a trance and saw the Lord speaking. 'Quick!' He said to me, 'leave Jerusalem immediately because they will not accept your testimony about me.'

'Lord,' I replied, 'these men know that I went from one synagogue to another to imprison and beat those who believe in you. And when the blood of your martyr Stephen was shed, I stood there giving my approval and guarding the clothes of those who were killing him.'

Then the Lord said, 'Go; I will send you far away to the Gentiles.' "(Verses 14-21)

Paul ends his testimony with what the Lord is doing now in his life.

The truth Paul shared with his audience is that Christ saved him, transformed his life, and was moving in him that very day. Paul wanted the crowd to realize the transformation that had occurred and to understand that he was now doing everything to live for Christ. So Paul first shared briefly about his life before Christ, then he shared how he came to Christ and how Christ transformed him. That was his testimony. *And that is your testimony.* Your testimony is to share your life before Christ, how you came to Christ and what Christ is doing in your life right *now*. Sounds simple, doesn't it? It is! Don't be intimidated. It is really much easier than you would think.

Now it's Your Turn

Our challenge to you right now is to think and pray about what your life was like before Christ, how you came to Christ, and how your life has been transformed. Take some time to ponder and pray about it. Then take a piece of paper and write out your personal testimony. It doesn't have to be long; limit it to one page, if you like. Then share your testimony with a parent, spouse, friend, or pastor. Writing out your testimony can be an exciting time for you to relive the day you asked Christ into your heart and began walking in obedience to Him. You can also include the day you were baptized if that differs from your day of acceptance. Just like memories one enjoys reliving, remembering and writing out your testimony can be a reviving time for you as you remember the joy and peace you found in the Lord.

Helpful Hints to Remember

Here is a list of "Do's" when sharing your testimony with another student, teacher, friend, or family member.

• Do remember if they reject what you share, they are rejecting the truth and not you.

• Do stay humble. Remember you are the Lord's tool, but He is the one who convicts the soul to repent.

• Do pray for the person before, during, and after you share with them.

• When you are with someone who is sharing the gospel, don't just watch–do pray!

111

Here is a list of "Don'ts" when sharing your testimony with another student, teacher, friend, or family member.

• Don't use Christian words that are hard to understand. (e.g. sanctified, converted.)

• Don't be too wordy. Be sensitive to God's leading with each individual and their present willingness to listen.

• Don't mention any church denomination in a negative way.

• Don't speak negatively about any other individual or group; however, be honest if a cult led you astray at one point.

• Don't give the impression that after your audience accepts Christ, life will be easy, and he or she will have no problems. Share how He helps you deal with problems when they come.

• Don't focus on stopping the sin, without first working to save the sinner.

• Don't "pressure" someone to pray to receive the Lord if they say they are not ready.

10

JUST DO SOMETHING!
The Many Opportunities that Escape Us Each Day

*"The rule for all of us is perfectly simple. Do not
waste time bothering whether you love your neighbor;
act as if you did. As soon as we do this we
find one of the great secrets. When you are behaving
as if you love someone, you will presently come to love him."*
—C.S. Lewis

Opportunities Right Next Door

Why is it that we don't take advantage of every opportunity to
share the gospel? I am asking that question of myself also. New neigh-
bors just moved in next door to us. We reached out to this family by
introducing ourselves, talking with the kids, and offering our help to
them if they needed it. Through our initial discussions, we suspected
one or both of them are from a religious background, but they do not
go to church or practice any faith. Then life got busy as it always does.
Brad and I were talking the other day and wondering why we have not
done more to reach out to them. We plan to do more and have already
decided to invite them to upcoming church activities. It is an opportunity God has placed right next door that we are going to take advantage
of . . . even if we should have done it sooner. What opportunities are
right next door, *or in your classroom or at the desk next to yours* that you
can take advantage of? Look at it this way. God has placed you in your
school, in your classes, at this time, for a reason. And that reason is to
share Him with those around you. Isn't that exciting when you think
about it? You have purpose! God did not create us randomly; rather,
He created us purposefully. He has a purpose for each and every one of
us. If you have any doubts about that, read Psalm 139.

A well-known quote by Saint Francis of Assisi is, "Preach the gospel at all times-use words if necessary." In other words, whatever our

position in life (student, teacher, parent, lawyer, school administrator, etc.) our goal should be to live our lives as Christ would. As we live our life to glorify Christ, we will be sharing with people through our actions, our reactions, our choices, and our words. Let that be our goal in our school, our workplace, our home, and our community.

What's The Message?

"Christian Rock. Isn't that an oxymoron?" That statement spoken sarcastically by the mom on the television show, "The Gilmore Girls" in one of their episodes is *mildly* indicative of how the media views Christians and the church. Whether it is the pastor character on "The Simpson's" or a token Catholic in name only on "Beverly Hills 90210," the same question can be asked of Christian characters in the media: What's the message? The message the media portrays of Christians and the church is usually one of weakness and irrelevance. Once in a while positive messages break through on shows like "Doc" and "Extreme Makeover, Home Edition." In general, however, religion on television is packaged in negative wrapping which gives many people a distorted view of God and religion, especially when it comes to programs children and teenagers watch. Media is so pervasive in our culture and in our children's lives that Christians, both young and old, have quite a challenge when they answer the call to evangelize in their schools. The truth of the matter is we live in a world in need of purpose, meaning, and truth. The message the media sends is generally misleading and Christians are responsible to set the record straight by sharing the truth of the Gospel.

A World in Need of Something

If you were to ask people if they are happy, many would say, "Yes, I am happy." But if you were to really press them on the topic, they might change their minds. They might think, "Well, actually, if I had a bigger house I think I would be much happier." Or, "If I were married I would be much happier." "If I were single I would be much happier." How about, "If I lived by the beach I would be really happy, or if I won the next lotto that would make me happy"? What do some people think would make them happy? Winning the lottery? Becoming famous or powerful? Finding the love of their life? Well, that doesn't seem to be the case. Take, for example, Harrison Ford. He is one of the greatest and most respected actors of our time. Money is definitely no problem. He is married and has children. He has one of the most famous faces in the world. During an interview a few years ago, Harrison Ford said to a reporter in response to her question about all that he had accomplished, "You only want what you ain't got." "What don't you have?" the reporter asked. "I don't have peace", he said. "If I die and I don't have peace, I'm really gonna be ticked off."

All people, even famous people, have an emptiness in their life if they do not know the Lord. Often people appear not to need anything, so we just pass them by, not considering the fact that they need the Lord also. The talented drama student; the shy, quiet student; the popular athlete; the rebellious troublemaker; the overzealous student; even the loner at school appears as if he or she does not want attention or acknowledgement. If people appear to not need anything, it is only because they are filling their lives with one thing after another in order to be happy. In fact, I believe that some people have fooled themselves into thinking they are happy. Brad once wrote a story, a sort of parable that speaks to the futility of gaining the whole world yet losing one's soul.

Lives Built of Sandcastles

It was the break of dawn. The tide had just gone out. An elderly man with long grey hair soon appeared on the beach. Though he had appeared on the beach many times before, few had ever taken note of him or his mission. Surveying the area, he pondered to find the best spot where his masterpiece would garner the most attention. It would be a masterpiece that would hopefully penetrate the soul of all who saw it.

Not wasting any time, the artist quickly unloaded all of his tools for sculpting. With a passion, he unwrapped the shovel and quickly began the task. Scoop after scoop the sand began to fly…higher and higher…and higher, until the scoops of sand had developed into a gigantic mound.

"Surely the others on the beach will begin to notice!" the artist thought. And notice they did.

As the artist piled on the last scoop, a building contractor on his way to a major construction site let forth a pity-filled sigh, "What a waste of time. Everyone knows that eventually the tide will return and wash his mound completely away!" And with that, the contractor hurried on to his nobler pursuits.

Soon after, the artist began to sculpt the castle portion of the work, meticulously carving the trim in a way that even the greatest architects of the world would have to take notice. And notice they did.

While finishing up the last part of the crown shingles, a very successful architect on his way to a new shopping center *did* take notice. "Incredible design!" he exclaimed. "What a shame he's spending so much valuable time on something that will surely be washed away!"

The artist continued his work non-stop throughout the early afternoon as he began to sculpt the bodies of the make-believe characters occupying the castle. Careful stroke after careful stroke, the artist tediously made sure the royal subjects would have the finest figures and stature that any human could hope for.

A group of college students on spring break headed for the gym and took notice of the figures. "Now that's exactly how I plan to look some day!" shouted one of the students. "You'll have to devote lots of time to obtain that!" another responded. As they walked away, they all agreed that it was unfortunate such figures would eventually be washed away. But it did not bother them; other good-looking models always seemed available on the newsstand.

The artist was in no way distracted by their comments. He had a mission and would continue to devote his heart and soul to it.

As the artist began to complete the township surrounding the castle, a local politician running for office who was most diligent to approach everyone on the beach with his campaign brochures, noticed he had yet to approach the artist. He leaned over to hand the artist one of his flyers, but the artist refused to allow anything or anyone to keep him from his mission. Disgusted that the artist refused to take notice of him, the politician quietly mumbled as he walked away, "How foolish can anyone be! He's building a kingdom that won't last but a few more hours!" After a few chuckles, the politician quickly returned to his timely endeavors.

116

Now it was time for the moat around the township. This was one of the more pleasant parts of the mission. You see, as the sun began to bake, the artist's feet enjoyed the soothing sensation of allowing the water-filled moat to cool his feet.

Just as he finished the drawbridge, a few high school students passed by. These students had passed by the artist many times before as they spent all of their spare time just basking in the sun for the ultimate in west coast relaxation. Feeling the hot sand on their toes, they noticed the voluminous moat with the cool ocean water swishing between the toes of the hurried artist.

"Wouldn't that be nice to have every day on the beach." commented one; "Lying in the sun while at the same time allowing your feet to rest in the moat. Now that would be a completely new sensation!" Bringing them back to reality, one of the others quickly reminded them what a waste of time it would be to construct such a project since the ocean would wash it away before sunset.

And sunset soon came. The ocean tide rushed in. As it did, the artist continued to work on the castle, glancing to see if any had taken notice of his work. Some had seemed to take notice, but not the way the artist had hoped. As the last of the sand castle washed away, the artist soon disappeared never to be seen on the beach again. Maybe someone, at some time, will allow the memory of his masterpiece to once again come to mind and his mission would then finally be fulfilled. For the artist knew one thing that many on the beach refused to learn: *How foolish it is to invest all that you have into something you cannot keep, then to give it all up for something you cannot lose.*

Many people think they are happy, depending on their circumstances, of course. But something will happen, sometime, to make them question the meaning of life and the purpose of their existence. It is for those times that God has called us to step in and share about the hope we have in Him. Regardless of our life's circumstances, He remains the same yesterday, today and forever, and He loves us. That is the answer. That is His message. That is our calling.

Do Not Underestimate Yourself

Right now you might be thinking there may be a lot of qualified people in this world, but you are not one of them. *Do not underestimate yourself or the power of God.* It is at the point that you do not think you are good enough, talented enough, or strong enough to be *ready.* "What? That makes no sense!" you might be thinking. But, it is at the point we realize we are not good enough to be used by God that God wants to use us. There is an old saying: He is not concerned about our ability, but about our availability. If we are not adequate enough to be used by God, then when He does use us, which He will do, if we let Him, then He will get all the glory. And that is the way it ought to be.

Brad openly shares that when he started the Pacific Justice Institute over seven years ago, he did not feel adequate to do so. He had been working for another non-profit organization doing the same type of work and was very content. He felt safe and secure and, as he puts it, had finally reached cruise control. "Watch out when you get to that point," he cautions. "God often likes to shake things up a bit." In 1997, Brad started Pacific Justice Institute because it was clear that this was exactly what God was calling him to do. There is a lot of work involved in starting something like this, but he felt confident he had everything planned out. If he worked all day and into the night, six and a half days a week, he thought he could make it work. That's the problem. It was not about Brad making it work. It was about God making it work. Thirty days after starting PJI, Brad got into a hit and run, head-on collision. He had to take time off to go to physical therapy, and for a while he had to work about half the hours because of the pain he was experiencing. What happened? God took the ministry and ran with it. There is a great peace in knowing that God raised up the Pacific Justice Institute. As Brad says, "It is His baby. He raised it up, and he can bring it down if he wants. I will just trust in Him." Now when tough times come or trials happen, Brad and his staff can have the peace that God is the one running the show, and they trust in Him for that.

In the same way, God wants to take you where you are and use you. It is in using you where you are that you will grow most in Him. If you were all-talented, all-strong and all-ready, you would not need God. So if you think you are inadequate to be used by Him, if you think God cannot use someone like you, congratulations. You are ready to be used by God. Ask Him to use you and watch things happen!

The Conclusion of the Matter

Once, when Brad was wondering about the state of our nation, he asked God a question that many of us have had on our minds at one time or another. The question he asked was, "Where is our nation headed, for a time of revival or a time of judgment and persecution?" Our world history is full of times of both revival and judgment. Trials and judgment often bring a nation that has turned away, back to God. In answer to Brad's question, God brought the story of Moses to his mind. As far as we know, when Moses and the Israelites came to the Red Sea and the waters were parted, they never questioned how long the waters would stay that way. They were not concerned about having time for a carnival or a garage sale. They simply obeyed God and took the opportunity as God gave it. They were faithful and walked through the waters that God had parted. In the same way, God has held back the waters for this nation. We are fortunate to live in a nation founded on religious freedom and the principles of God's Word. It is by His will that He has held back the waters of judgment on this nation. Just as it was for the Israelites, the question for us is not how long the waters for this great nation will be parted. Rather, the question is whether we will be faithful and obedient to God and take advantage of that freedom to evangelize as He has called us to. To be faithful and obedient to Him is all that God asks. He will take care of the rest.

INFORMATION ABOUT PACIFIC JUSTICE INSTITUTE

Reading this book has informed you of some of the work the Pacific Justice Institute does. In this section we will summarize how PJI got started, its mission, and how this ministry helps parents and Christians in school, work, churches, and more.

Pacific Justice Institute works with over 1000 affiliate attorneys nationwide. These attorneys work with PJI pro bono, so that the ever-increasing requests for assistance can be answered without charge. In the year prior to the third printing of this book, PJI had over 2000 requests for assistance.

About the PJI President

Brad Dacus served as Legislative Assistant to U.S. Senator Phil Gramm and went on to receive his Juris Doctorate from the University of Texas School of Law. For the next five years, Brad coordinated religious freedom and parental rights cases throughout the Western states. In 1997, he founded Pacific Justice Institute where he serves as President and continues to defend liberties and parental rights, both on the west coast and throughout the country.

Brad Dacus has been a featured guest at Focus on the Family's "Heart of the Physician" Conference, Teacher's Conference, and Attorney's Conference. He participates weekly on several radio talk-show interviews throughout the country and can be heard giving "The Legal Edge" on numerous radio stations. He has also appeared on "Good Morning America," "The Today Show," "CNN," "Hannity and Colmes," "MSNBC," "Dateline," and many times on "The O'Reilly Factor," among others. Brad Dacus has participated in a variety of public speaking opportunities including two debates against the President of the ACLU (American Civil Liberties Union). He has also squared off against the President of "Americans United for Separation of Church and State." Twice he has made presentations to the American Bar Association regarding PJI's many church defense cases and the impact of RLUIPA (Religious Land Use and Institutionalized Persons Act). He has testified numerous times before the California State Legislature, has guest lectured at Stanford University School of Law and speaks regularly at churches, conferences, and universities throughout the United States.

Mission and Goals—Case Examples

The mission of Pacific Justice Institute is to see that all those who need help get it in regards to religious freedom and parental rights. This book provides insight into a number of the school cases the Pacific Justice Institute has dealt with. They do, however, take a number of different types of cases, including religious harassment in the workplace, defending churches and private schools that are discriminated against, and the right of parents to guide the education of their children. The following examples show the wide variety of cases the Pacific Justice Institute defends in order to preserve our constitutional rights.

Work-related Cases

Mark Smith* is an employee at NASA in Silicon Valley, California. Through the center-wide email system, employees regularly send out information regarding various community activities, including AIDS Awareness Day, etc. Mark wanted to send a message about the National Day of Prayer and a voluntary prayer event that was approaching. He was told he was not allowed to do so because of (you guessed it) the "separation of church and state". Mark did not just give up on his idea. Instead, he called Pacific Justice Institute to see if there was something that could be done. One of the in-house attorneys contacted the legal division of NASA, explained where the law had been violated, and asked that the matter be resolved quickly. The matter was resolved immediately, Mark was able to send the e-mail message, and the event went off without a hitch.

Other cases include preserving the right to wear religious jewelry or display religious material in an office cubicle, and the list goes on and on. The bottom line is that Christians should not have to always compromise or accept harassment in the workplace, whether involving a large issue or a small one.

Para-Church Ministries

Valley Christian Home is a wonderful home in Southern California that takes care of widows and widowers. What horrible thing did this home do to cause the Fair Housing Authority to come after them? In their yellow page ad they put the words, Christian environment. The Fair Housing Authority said they could not do this because the Home did not minister to members of only one denomination, but many. Do not try to make any sense of it. The government wanted Valley Christian Home to pay a large fine, take those words out of the yellow page advertisement, plus require all of their employees to attend a "sensitivity training" workshop. Instead of giving in to the demands of the city, they called the Pacific Justice Institute. After two years of litigation, Pacific Justice Institute had a wonderful victory. Valley Christian Home did not have to remove their advertisement; did not have to pay the fine, and did not have to send personnel to the sensitivity workshop. That is just one example of a para-church ministry that PJI has helped.

Churches/Private Christian Schools

Near San Diego, California, a church is bursting at the seams. They have so many ministries and God is growing their church in such a way that they are ready to move into a larger facility. They have found a perfect place to move, in the city where God has called them, where space would not be a problem, and the ministry would be fruitful. They spoke with the owner of this facility, and the owner was willing to sell. Here we have a buyer willing and able to buy, and a seller willing to sell. What could be the problem? After all this is a privately owned facility; therefore, everything should have gone smoothly. And it did until it was brought before the city council. The city council decided they did not want a church there. Is it because of a safety or health issue? No. How about a disruption to the community? No, actually a church, especially one as large as this one, would bring social services and business to the surrounding community. What was the problem? The city council voted three to two against the sale of this property because, instead of a church, they wanted "a village" at that property. The city council preferred an area with shops and boutiques to attract tourists. (No offense to this particular community, but it is not exactly what could be called a tourist town.) The church called Pacific Justice Institute because their freedoms were being violated. PJI agreed to take

*Name has been changed to protect privacy

on the case, and at the time of this writing, the case is still in litigation. We pray for victory, but whatever happens, both the church and PJI trust in God for the outcome of this case.

This is just one of *many* examples of church cases Pacific Justice Institute is defending. The Religious Land Use and Institutionalized Persons Act (RLUIPA) was passed in 2000 and signed into law. This law provides great protection for churches and private Christian schools and colleges. This legislation is a great tool for PJI to use to defend religious institutions.

Freedom of Speech and Patriotism

We at the Pacific Justice Institute have always taken cases involving free speech and patriotism. Since the tragedy of September 11th we have received many calls similar to the examples we have included in this section. It is our goal to continue to fight for every child's right to neither hide their faith nor their love of country.

Students Prevented From Wearing Patriotic Pin

A grandparent of two boys who were told by their high school teacher that they were not allowed to wear patriotic pins because of the school district's "gang paraphernalia" policy contacted the Pacific Justice Institute. The pins consisted of an American flag and the words "God Bless America." According to the grandfather, the boys were allegedly threatened with suspension if they wore their patriotic symbols again. After contacting the school district in Anaheim, California, and following up with a legal opinion letter, one of our attorneys was assured that the teacher had been acting outside the policies of the school district. The district also promised to inform its entire faculty at the upcoming faculty meeting as to the importance of respecting the rights of students to wear patriotic symbols. "I am very grateful for the Pacific Justice Institute and how quickly they resolved this matter," said the grandfather. "Our goal was that my two grandsons not be severely punished for expressing their love of country."

Student Allowed to Keep "In God We Trust" on School Project

Due to a misunderstanding of what the law allows in schools, a teacher at a public high school in Washington State required one of his students to remove the words "In God We Trust" from a piece of patriotic artwork the student had submitted for public display. The teacher apparently believed it was necessary to censor the student's reference to God in order to comply with the so-called "wall of separation" between church and state.

Shortly thereafter, the student's mother contacted us to request some information on what her son's rights were. Upon providing this information to her in the form of a legal opinion letter, the student's mother presented it to the school and teacher, who both subsequently changed their positions and allowed the reference to God to remain in the student's project.

Home School/Child Protective Services

Pacific Justice Institute is committed to assisting parents who home school and families who are threatened by CPS (Child Protective Services). We provide emergency counseling to non-abusive parents when social services has threatened to remove children from the home, and we furnish specific information on what parents can do to mitigate the charges. We have particular expertise if the parents are home schooling or using *acceptable forms* of corporal punishment. (We understand that there are definitely abuse cases out there that are indefensible.) Corporal punishment, on the other hand, is simply appropriate spanking to discipline the child, and only when reasonably necessary.

One of the goals of Pacific Justice Institute is to see major changes in legislation regarding Child Protective Services. In states like Texas and Oklahoma, parents are given a jury of their peers before their children are taken away permanently. Also, any interview of a child is to be taped for accuracy. This is not the law in California unfortunately, as it should be. Reforming this system would be a victory for all parents in the state of California and other states with similar systems.

Special Projects

Pastors' Legal Seminars

Pacific Justice Institute hosts legal seminars for pastors, conducted by PJI's well-informed legal staff and a variety of invited speakers. Covering a wide range of issues, these three-hour seminars educate pastors substantively on their legal rights and let them know that if they ever need legal representation, PJI stands ready to serve them without charge. These events are often co-hosted by a Christian college, ministerial association or church and usually include breakfast or lunch.

Reclaim Your Workplace: The Religious Freedom Rights of Employers and Employees

Pacific Justice Institute is pleased to offer both a booklet and a presentation to business owners and CEO's entitled Reclaim Your Workplace, which clarifies the religious freedom rights of employers and employees. Christian business owners and CEO's do not want to hide their faith in the workplace, yet often do not know what the law says on the issue. This informative booklet and presentation opens up the eyes of business owners and frees them to share their faith with their employees in a manner that is not in violation of the law.

Media Events

Pacific Justice Institute does frequent radio and TV interviews nationwide (See "About the PJI President" above), and PJI's "Legal Edge" one-minute broadcast is heard weekly on dozens of radio stations. For information and in order to have this program aired on your local radio station, call Pacific Justice Institute.

In addition to periodic live interviews for Focus on the Family, PJI also does commentary which appears monthly on Focus's weekend show, airing on 600 radio stations.

Internship Program

PJI sponsors an internship program for college students and law students. Students come to PJI from all over the country and are given substantive responsibility which stretches their skills and expands their understanding of the latest challenges.

California School Project

PJI trains and provides resources to this Campus Crusade ministry headed up by Warren Willis (wpwillis@aol.com). This project involves college students sponsoring revival rallies on public school campuses throughout Los Angeles, addressing, through testimonials, the topics of drugs, alcohol, homosexuality and Christian apologetics. To date, revival rallies have been sponsored on more than 3 dozen campuses in the L.A. area. PJI is willing to help other ministries put on rallies at their local schools.

The Celebration of Justice

The Celebration of Justice event honors attorneys, community leaders and media personalities who have made significant contributions to the community in the areas of faith, family and freedom and who have exhibited the values of truth and justice in their lives and work. This is a gala event and is presented twice annually, in Sacramento in the fall, and in Irvine in the spring. Some keynote speakers who have appeared at these events are former U.S. Attorney General Ed Meese, Judge Roy Moore, California State Senator Tom McClintock, and media personalities Alan Keyes and Cal Thomas.

Attorney Seminar Training

Pacific Justice Institute sponsors continuing education seminars for attorneys. These seminars train attorneys practically in the defense of religious freedom and parental rights.

The Church and Politics: What Pastors and Churches Can Do to Affect Public Policy with Christian Principles

This booklet provides you with information about what a church can do to advocate Biblically based positions on issues and legislation while still preserving its tax-exempt status. It clarifies the legal opportunities available to pastors and churches to register voters, host candidate forums, distribute voter materials, and generally advance Christian principles in government and public policy.

Choose Charity

As mentioned in chapter seven of this book, teachers can have all of their union dues given to a charity instead of to their union. This applies to anyone who works for a union, including the government, a supermarket, an automobile plant, etc. If you have to pay union dues and are interested in the Choose Charity program, read the Choose Charity portion of chapter seven, then contact our office for more information.

Public Education: Religious Rights and Values in California Schools

Designed to be a resource for those concerned with the public school system, this booklet summarizes some of the issues discussed in this book (Reclaim Your School), plus additional topics such as confidential medical releases and teacher initiated political/religious speech. Directed toward School Boards and administrators, as well as parents, it encapsulates the religious freedom rights and responsibilities of parents and students, including the rights parents have to direct the education of their children.

Opt-Out Forms

As discussed in Chapter 6, these forms require schools to notify parents before the presentation of certain objectionable subjects so that parents may review instructional materials, and allow parents to have their children excused from such presentations. A sample opt-out form is provided in Appendix 1, and on our website:
http://www.pacificjustice.org/resources/forms/sexopt.cfm

Speakers Bureau

PJI offers dynamic speakers on a variety of subjects, including clarifying the legality of parents' rights, church rights and evangelizing in public schools. In addition, Brad is always eager to speak at churches, especially at Sunday morning services, to present his message that will encourage and equip Christians to share their faith boldly.

What You Can Do to Help

As you can see, Pacific Justice Institute takes on a variety of cases to help parents, employees, business owners, churches and more. Your prayers and support are what make all of this possible. If you would like to keep updated on what PJI is doing, sign up on the internet at www.pacificjustice.org. You can sign up to receive press releases and newsletters to keep up with our current cases. Pacific Justice Institute, a non-profit 501(c)(3) organization, does all of its work free of charge. Knowing how expensive litigation is, people often ask how this is possible. It is possible because of individual donations from people like you. We also have some churches that support what we are doing.

APPENDIX 1
Sample Union Dues Letter

Dear_____ (Union):

My religious beliefs prevent me from contributing to this union. (At this point you must explain your beliefs. Feel free to quote scripture, religious experiences, and/or religious reasoning.)

In accordance with section 701(j) of Title VII of the Civil Rights Act, I ask that you divert the entirety of my union dues to the following non-profit charities:

_____

_____

I hereby declare, under penalty of perjury, that the above is true and correct.

Thank you for your reasonable accommodation of my sincerely held religious beliefs.

Sincerely,

_____

(Your name)

cc: Brad Dacus, Esq.

(Before sending this letter to your union, please send it first to the Pacific Justice Institute so it can be reviewed without charge.)

---

* Please note: You should be aware that under Federal Law, your union has the right to designate three charities for you to choose from when diverting your dues. If they do not designate any, then you may divert your dues to the nonprofit, non-labor, non-religious charity of your choice.

Sample School Opt-Out Form

The Opt-Out Form may be found additionally from PJI's website, at:

http://www.pacificjustice.org/resources/forms/sexopt.cfm

CALIFORNIA EXCUSE OF PUPIL FROM OBJECTIONABLE EDUCATION

To: School Board Members, Superintendent, Principal, Teachers, Counselors and Staff of the _____ School District.

Cc: Pacific Justice Institute
P.O. Box 276600
Sacramento, CA 95827
pji@pacificjustice.org

I, _____, am the parent or legal guardian of _____ , who is enrolled in the _____ grade at _____ _____ (school).

This letter serves as legal notice that I am exercising my rights under 20 U.S.C. 1232(h) and the California Education Code (Educ.C.), including but not limited to, Sections 221.5, 51100, 51101, 51501, 51513, and 51937-51939, to exempt my child from objectionable education.

Pursuant to Educ.C. § 51938, I, as a parent or guardian of a pupil, am exercising my right to excuse my child from all or part of comprehensive sexual health education, HIV/AIDS prevention education, and assessments related to that education.

Additionally, please notify me, as per the requirements of Educ.C. § 51938(a), "about instruction in comprehensive sexual health education and HIV/AIDS prevention education and research on pupil health behaviors and risks planned for the coming year." The notice must include all of the following:

(1) Assurance that written and audio visual educational materials used in comprehensive sexual health education and HIV/AIDS prevention education are available for inspection.

(2) Whether the comprehensive sexual health education or HIV/ AIDS prevention education will be taught by school district personnel or by outside consultants.

(3) Any information explaining my right as a parent or guardian to request a copy of these instructional materials

(4) That I, as the parent or guardian, may request in writing that my child not receive comprehensive sexual health education or HIV/ AIDS prevention education.

In addition, pursuant to the policy adopted by the District under Educ.C. § 51101(b)(G), I wish to participate in any and all "decisions relating to the education of [my] child" in the following areas (Insert subjects, e.g,):

1. Family life, health, or human sexuality education;
2. Homosexuality, lesbianism, bi-sexuality, transgender or transsexual issues;
3. Gender identity, sexual orientation, sexual preference; and,
4. Any alternatives to monogamous heterosexual marriage.

Before any of the above topics are presented to my child, please take notice that I am exercising my rights under the California Education Code to do the following: (1) examine the curriculum materials regarding said topics (Educ.C. § 51101(a)(8); and, (2) meet with the instructor and principal to discuss the presentation of these topics to my child (Educ.C. § 51101(a)(2).

Furthermore, in accordance with Title 20 U.S.C. 1232(h) and Educ.C. § 51513, unless you obtain my express written consent for each occurrence, you are not to administer any test, questionnaire, survey, or examination containing any questions about my child[ren]'s personal beliefs or practices in sex, family life, morality, and religion, or any questions about my child[ren]'s parents' or guardians' beliefs and practices in sex, family life, morality, and religion. Additionally, as per Educ.C. § 51101(a)(13), I wish to receive information about any psychological testing the school does involving my child prior to its administration. Unless I provide express written consent, I am denying permission to give any such test.

This restriction applies to all agents of the school and the school district, including, but not limited to, teachers, teacher aides, administrators, school counselors, school health personnel, special guests or presenters, California

Department of Education or other state departments or their agents, or anyone speaking or acting on behalf of the school or school district.

Furthermore, this restriction shall be applicable whether the pupil is on school grounds, or elsewhere.

This exemption requirement additionally applies to all writings as defined by California Evidence Code § 250, including, but not limited to:

1. Classroom instruction, presentations, and campus displays;
2. Reading assignments, class discussions, homework assignments;
3. Photographs, films, filmstrips, slides, DVDs, CDs, video tapes, audio tapes, MP3, movies, projector images;
4. CD-Roms, Internet programs and other computer-related activities;
5. Books, magazines, newspapers, and other written or printed material;
6. Assemblies, field trips, theatrical or musical performances; or
7. Extracurricular activities and individual or group activities.

Based on the foregoing notice, I respectfully request to be notified in writing at least 14 days in advance of all future instruction, events, activities, etc., from which my child may need to be exempted so that I may work with you in providing alternate accommodations for my child's education. This request is made based on our family's sincerely held religious beliefs, as well as the need to protect my child from possible physical, emotional, or psychological harm or trauma.

I request that the principal and all teachers or other agents of the school district who are involved with the education of the above named pupil[s] be informed of this legal, written notice, and that they be made aware of the penalties associated with knowingly violating my rights as set forth in this document. This form supersedes any prior exemption or authorization forms you may have on file for the above-referenced pupil[s].

In order to assure that this form is on file and the appropriate individuals have been notified, please acknowledge receipt and filing of this document in writing. Thank you for your cooperation.

Thank you for respecting my family's moral convictions in these matters. If you have any questions, please feel free to contact me at your convenience.

Signed: _____

Date: _____

Address: _____

_____

Daytime/Evening Phone Number(s): _____

_____

APPENDIX 2

20 USC 4071

TITLE 20—EDUCATION

CHAPTER 52—EDUCATION FOR ECONOMIC SECURITY

SUBCHAPTER VIII—EQUAL ACCESS

Sec. 4071. Denial of equal access prohibited

(a) Restriction of limited open forum on the basis of religious, political, philosophical, or other speech content prohibited

It shall be unlawful for any public secondary school which receives Federal financial assistance and which has a limited open forum to deny equal access or a fair opportunity to, or discriminate against, any students who wish to conduct a meeting within that limited open forum on the basis of the religious, political, philosophical, or other content of the speech at such meetings.

(b) "Limited open forum" defined

A public secondary school has a limited open forum whenever such school grants an offering to or opportunity for one or more non-curriculum related student groups to meet on school premises during non-instructional time.

(c) Fair opportunity criteria

Schools shall be deemed to offer a fair opportunity to students who wish to conduct a meeting within its limited open forum if such school uniformly provides that—
(1) The meeting is voluntary and student-initiated;
(2) There is no sponsorship of the meeting by the school, the government, or its agents or employees;
(3) Employees or agents of the school or government are present at religious meetings only in a non-participatory capacity;

(4) The meeting does not materially and substantially interfere with the orderly conduct of educational activities within the school; and

(5) Non-school persons may not direct, conduct, control, or regularly attend activities of student groups.

(d) Construction of subchapter with respect to certain rights

Nothing in this subchapter shall be construed to authorize the United States or any State or political subdivision thereof—

(1) To influence the form or content of any prayer or other religious activity;

(2) To require any person to participate in prayer or other religious activity;

(3) To expend public funds beyond the incidental cost of providing the space for student-initiated meetings;

(4) To compel any school agent or employee to attend a school meeting if the content of the speech at the meeting is contrary to the beliefs of the agent or employee;

(5) To sanction meetings that are otherwise unlawful;

(6) To limit the rights of groups of students which are not of a specified numerical size; or

(7) To abridge the constitutional rights of any person.

(e) Federal financial assistance to schools unaffected

Notwithstanding the availability of any other remedy under the Constitution or the laws of the United States, nothing in this subchapter shall be construed to authorize the United States to deny or withhold Federal financial assistance to any school.

(f) Authority of schools with respect to order, discipline, well-being, and attendance concerns

Nothing in this subchapter shall be construed to limit the authority of the school, its agents or employees, to maintain order and discipline on school premises, to protect the well-being of students and faculty, and to assure that attendance of students at meetings is voluntary.

(Pub. L. 98-377, title VIII, Sec. 802, Aug. 11, 1984, 98 Stat. 1302.)

APPENDIX 3

Memorandum for the U.S. Secretary of Education and the U.S. Attorney General

SUBJECT: Religious Expression in Public Schools

Religious freedom is perhaps the most precious of all American liberties—called by many our "first freedom." Many of the first European settlers in North America sought refuge from religious persecution in their native countries. Since that time, people of faith and religious institutions have played a central role in the history of this Nation. In the First Amendment, our Bill of Rights recognizes the twin pillars of religious liberty: the constitutional protection for the free exercise of religion, and the constitutional prohibition of the establishment of religion by the state. Our Nation's founders knew that religion helps to give our people the character without which a democracy cannot survive. Our founders also recognized the need for a space of freedom between government and the people—that the government must not be permitted to coerce the conscience of any individual or group.

In the over 200 years since the First Amendment was included in our Constitution, religion and religious institutions have thrived throughout the United States. In 1993, I was proud to reaffirm the historic place of religion when I signed the Religious Freedom Restoration Act, which restores a high legal standard to protect the exercise of religion from being inappropriately burdened by government action. In the greatest traditions of American citizenship, a broad coalition of individuals and organizations came together to support the fullest protection for religious practice and expression.

RELIGIOUS EXPRESSION IN PUBLIC SCHOOLS

I share the concern and frustration that many Americans feel about situations where the protections accorded by the First Amendment are not recognized or understood. This problem has manifested itself in our Nation's public schools. It appears that some school officials, teachers, and parents have assumed that religious expression of any type is either inappropriate, or forbidden altogether, in public schools.

As our courts have reaffirmed, however, nothing in the First Amendment converts our public schools into religion-free zones, or requires all religious expression to be left behind at the schoolhouse door. While the government may not use schools to coerce the consciences of our students, or to convey official endorsement of religion, the government's schools also may not discriminate against private religious expression during the school day.

I have been advised by the Department of Justice and the Department of Education that the First Amendment permits—and protects—a greater degree of religious expression in public schools than many Americans may now understand. The Departments of Justice and Education have advised me that, while application may depend upon specific factual contexts and will require careful consideration in particular cases, the following principles are among those that apply to religious expression in our schools:

Student prayer and religious discussion:

The Establishment Clause of the First Amendment does not prohibit purely private religious speech by students. Students therefore have the same right to engage in individual or group prayer and religious discussion during the school day as they do to engage in other comparable activity. For example, students may read their Bibles or other scriptures, say grace before meals, and pray before tests to the same extent they may engage in comparable non-disruptive activities. Local school authorities possess substantial discretion to impose rules of order and other pedagogical restrictions on student activities, but they may not structure or administer such rules to discriminate against religious activity or speech.

Generally, students may pray in a non-disruptive manner when not engaged in school activities or instruction, and subject to the rules that normally pertain in the applicable setting. Specifically, students in informal settings, such as cafeterias and hallways, may pray and discuss their religious views with each other, subject to the same rules of order as apply to other student activities and speech. Students may also speak to, and attempt to persuade, their peers about religious topics just as they do with regard to political topics. School officials, however, should intercede to stop student speech that constitutes harassment aimed at a student or a group of students.

Students may also participate in before or after school events with religious content, such as "see you at the flag pole" gatherings, on the same terms as they may participate in other non-curriculum activities on school premises. School officials may neither discourage nor encourage participation in such an event.

The right to engage in voluntary prayer or religious discussion free from discrimination does not include the right to have a captive audience to listen, or to compel other students to participate. Teachers and school administrators should ensure that no student is in any way coerced to participate in religious activity.

Graduation prayer and baccalaureates:

Under current Supreme Court decisions, school officials may not mandate or organize prayer at graduation, nor organize religious baccalaureate ceremonies. If a school generally opens its facilities to private groups, it must make its facilities available on the same terms to organizers of privately sponsored religious baccalaureate services. A school may not extend preferential treatment to baccalaureate ceremonies and may in some instances be obliged to disclaim official endorsement of such ceremonies.

Official neutrality regarding religious activity:

Teachers and school administrators, when acting in those capacities, are representatives of the state and are prohibited by the establishment clause from soliciting or encouraging religious activity, and from participating in such activity with students. Teachers and administrators also are prohibited from discouraging activity because of its religious content, and from soliciting or encouraging antireligious activity.

Teaching about religion:

Public schools may not provide religious instruction, but they may teach *about* religion, including the Bible or other scripture: the history of religion, comparative religion, the Bible (or other scripture) as literature, and the role of religion in the history of the United States and other countries all are permissible public school subjects. Similarly, it is permissible to consider religious influences on art, music, literature, and social studies. Although public schools may teach about religious holidays, including their religious aspects, and may celebrate the secular aspects of holidays, schools may not observe holidays as religious events or promote such observance by students.

Student assignments:

Students may express their beliefs about religion in the form of homework, artwork, and other written and oral assignments free of discrimination based on the religious content of their submissions. Such home and classroom work should be judged by ordinary academic standards of substance and relevance, and against other legitimate pedagogical concerns identified by the school.

Religious literature:

Students have a right to distribute religious literature to their school-mates on the same terms as they are permitted to distribute other literature that is unrelated to school curriculum or activities. Schools may impose the same reasonable time, place, and manner or other constitutional restrictions on distribution of religious literature as they do on non-school literature generally, but they may not single out religious literature for special regulation.

Religious excusals:

Subject to applicable State laws, schools enjoy substantial discretion to excuse individual students from lessons that are objectionable to the student or students' parents on religious or other conscientious grounds. School officials may neither encourage nor discourage students from availing themselves of an excusal option. Under the Religious Freedom Restoration Act, if it is proved that particular lessons substantially burden a student's free exercise of religion, and if the school cannot prove a compelling interest in requiring attendance, the school would be legally required to excuse the student.

Released time:

Subject to applicable State laws, schools have the discretion to dismiss students to off-premises religious instruction, provided that schools do not encourage or discourage participation or penalize those who do not attend. Schools may not allow religious instruction by outsiders on school premises during the school day.

Teaching values:

Though schools must be neutral with respect to religion, they may play an active role with respect to teaching civic values and virtue, and the moral code that holds us together as a community. The fact that some of these values are held also by religions does not make it unlawful to teach them in school.

Student garb:

Students may display religious messages on items of clothing to the same extent that they are permitted to display other comparable messages. Religious messages may not be singled out for suppression, but rather are subject to the same rules as generally apply to comparable messages. When wearing particular attire, such as yarmulkes and head scarves, during the school day is part of students' religious practice, under the Religious Freedom Restoration Act, schools generally may not prohibit the wearing of such items.

I hereby direct the Secretary of Education, in consultation with the Attorney General, to use appropriate means to ensure that public school districts and school officials in the United States are informed, by the start of the coming school year, of the principles set forth above.

THE EQUAL ACCESS ACT

The Equal Access Act is designed to ensure that, consistent with the First Amendment, student religious activities are accorded the same access to public school facilities as are student secular activities. Based on decisions of the Federal courts, as well as its interpretations of the Act, the Department of Justice has advised me of its position that the Act should be interpreted as providing, among other things, that:

General provisions:

Student religious groups at public secondary schools have the same right of access to school facilities as is enjoyed by other comparable student groups. Under the Equal Access Act, a school receiving Federal funds that allows one or more student non-curriculum-related clubs to meet on its premises during non-instructional time may not refuse access to student religious groups.

Prayer services and worship exercises covered:

A meeting, as defined and protected by the Equal Access Act, may include a prayer service, Bible reading, or other worship exercise.

Equal access to means of publicizing meetings:

A school receiving Federal funds must allow student groups meeting under the Act to use the school media—including the public address system, the school newspaper, and the school bulletin board—to announce their meetings on the same terms as other non-curriculum-related student groups are allowed to use the school media. Any policy concerning the use of school media must be applied to all non-curriculum-related student groups in a non-discriminatory matter. Schools, however, may inform students that certain groups are not school sponsored.

Lunch-time and recess covered:

A school creates a limited open forum under the Equal Access Act, triggering equal access rights for religious groups, when it allows students to meet during their lunch periods or other non-instructional time during the school day, as well as when it allows students to meet before and after the school day.

I hereby direct the Secretary of Education, in consultation with the Attorney General, to use appropriate means to ensure that public school districts and school officials in the United States are informed, by the start of the coming school year, of these interpretations of the Equal Access Act.

Signed: William J. Clinton
July 12, 1995

APPENDIX 4

20 U.S.C. Section 1232h ("Hatch Amendment")

(a) Inspection of instructional materials by parents or guardians

All instructional materials, including teacher's manuals, films, tapes, or other supplementary material which will be used in connection with any survey, analysis, or evaluation as part of any applicable program shall be available for inspection by the parents or guardians of the children.

(b) Limits on survey, analysis, or evaluations

No student shall be required, as part of any applicable program, to submit to a survey, analysis, or evaluation that reveals information concerning—

(1)   political affiliations;

(2)   mental and psychological problems potentially embarrassing to the student or his family;

(3)   sex behavior and attitudes;

(4)   illegal, anti-social, self-incriminating and demeaning behavior;

(5)   critical appraisals of other individuals with whom respondents have close family relationships;

(6) legally recognized privileged or analogous relationships, such as those of lawyers, physicians, and ministers; or

(7) income (other than that required by law to determine eligibility for participation in a program or for receiving financial assistance under such program), without the prior consent of the student (if the student is an adult or emancipated minor), or in the case of an unemancipated minor, without the prior written consent of the parent.

(c) Notice

Educational agencies and institutions shall give parents and students effective notice of their rights under this section.

(d) Enforcement

The Secretary shall take such action as the Secretary determines appropriate to enforce this section, except that action to terminate assistance provided under an applicable program shall be taken only if the Secretary determines that—

(1) there has been a failure to comply with such section; and

(2) compliance with such section cannot be secured by voluntary means.

(e) Office and review board

The Secretary shall establish or designate an office and review board within the Department of Education to investigate, process, review, and adjudicate violations of the rights established under this section.

APPENDIX 5

Guidance on Constitutionally Protected Prayer in Public Elementary and Secondary Schools

Introduction

Secretary's Letter on Constitutionally Protected Prayer in Public Elementary and Secondary Schools

Dear Colleague:

As part of the implementation of the No Child Left Behind Act of 2001 (NCLB), I am issuing guidance today on constitutionally protected prayer in public elementary and secondary schools. The purpose of this guidance is to provide State educational agencies (SEAs), local educational agencies (LEAs) and the public with information on this important topic. The guidance also sets forth and explains the responsibilities of SEAs and LEAs with respect to this aspect of the NCLB Act. Most significantly, as a condition of receiving funds under the Elementary and Secondary Education Act (ESEA), an LEA must certify in writing to its SEA that it has no policy that prevents, or otherwise denies participation in, constitutionally protected prayer in public schools as set forth in this guidance.

The guidance clarifies the rights of students to pray in public schools. As stated in the guidance, "...the First Amendment forbids religious activity that is sponsored by the government but protects religious activity that is initiated by private individuals" such as students. Therefore, "[a]mong other things, students may read their Bibles or other scriptures, say grace before meals, and pray or study religious materials with fellow students during recess, the lunch hour, or other noninstructional time to the same extent that they may engage in nonreligious activities." Public schools should not be hostile to the religious rights of their students and their families.

At the same time, school officials may not "compel students to participate in prayer or other religious activities." Nor may teachers, school administrators and other school employees, when acting in their official capacities as representatives of the state, encourage or discourage prayer, or participate in such activities with students.

145

In these challenging times, it is more important than ever to recognize the freedoms we have. I hope that this guidance can contribute to a common understanding of the meaning of the First Amendment in the public school setting. I encourage you to distribute this guidance widely in your community and to discuss its contents and importance with school administrators, teachers, parents, and students.

Sincerely,
Rod Paige

Section 9524 of the Elementary and Secondary Education Act ("ESEA") of 1965, as amended by the No Child Left Behind Act of 2001, requires the Secretary to issue guidance on constitutionally protected prayer in public elementary and secondary schools. In addition, Section 9524 requires that, as a condition of receiving ESEA funds, a local educational agency ("LEA") must certify in writing to its State educational agency ("SEA") that it has no policy that prevents, or otherwise denies participation in, constitutionally protected prayer in public schools as set forth in this guidance.

The purpose of this guidance is to provide SEAs, LEAs, and the public with information on the current state of the law concerning constitutionally protected prayer in the public schools, and thus to clarify the extent to which prayer in public schools is legally protected. This guidance also sets forth the responsibilities of SEAs and LEAs with respect to Section 9524 of the ESEA. As required by the Act, this guidance has been jointly approved by the Office of the General Counsel in the Department of Education and the Office of Legal Counsel in the Department of Justice as reflecting the current state of the law. It will be made available on the Internet through the Department of Education's web site (www.ed.gov). The guidance will be updated on a biennial basis, beginning in September 2004, and provided to SEAs, LEAs, and the public.

The Section 9524 Certification Process

In order to receive funds under the ESEA, an LEA must certify in writing to its SEA that no policy of the LEA prevents, or otherwise denies participation in, constitutionally protected prayer in public elementary and secondary schools as set forth in this guidance. An LEA must provide this certification to the SEA by October 1, 2002, and by October 1 of each subsequent year during which the LEA participates in an ESEA program. However, as a transitional matter, given the timing of this guidance, the initial certification must be provided by an LEA to the SEA by March 15, 2003. The SEA should establish a process by which LEAs may provide the necessary certification. There is no specific Federal form that an LEA must use in providing this certification to its SEA. The certification may be provided as part of the application process for ESEA programs, or separately, and in whatever form the SEA finds most appropriate, as long as the certification is in writing and clearly states that the LEA has no policy that prevents, or otherwise denies participation in, constitutionally protected prayer in public elementary and secondary schools as set forth in this guidance.

By November 1 of each year, starting in 2002, the SEA must send to the Secretary a list of those LEAs that have not filed the required certification or against which complaints have been made to the SEA that the LEA is not in compliance with this guidance. However, as a transitional matter, given the timing of this guidance, the list otherwise due November 1, 2002, must be sent to the Secretary by April 15, 2003. This list should be sent to:

Office of Elementary and Secondary Education
Attention: Jeanette Lim
U.S. Department of Education
400 Maryland Avenue, S.W.
Washington, D.C. 20202

The SEA's submission should describe what investigation or enforcement action the SEA has initiated with respect to each listed LEA and the status of the investigation or action. The SEA should not send the LEA certifications to the Secretary, but should maintain these records in accordance with its usual records retention policy.

Enforcement of Section 9524:

LEAs are required to file the certification as a condition of receiving funds under the ESEA. If an LEA fails to file the required certification, or files it in bad faith, the SEA should ensure compliance in accordance with its regular enforcement procedures. The Secretary considers an LEA to have filed a certification in bad faith if the LEA files the certification even though it has a policy that prevents, or otherwise denies participation in, constitutionally protected prayer in public elementary and secondary schools as set forth in this guidance.

The General Education Provisions Act ("GEPA") authorizes the Secretary to bring enforcement actions against recipients of Federal education funds that are not in compliance with the law. Such measures may include withholding funds until the recipient comes into compliance. Section 9524 provides the Secretary with specific authority to issue and enforce orders with respect to an LEA that fails to provide the required certification to its SEA or files the certification in bad faith.

Overview of Governing Constitutional Principles

The relationship between religion and government in the United States is governed by the First Amendment to the Constitution, which both prevents the government from establishing religion and protects privately initiated religious expression and activities from government interference and discrimination. (1) The First Amendment thus establishes certain limits on the conduct of public school officials as it relates to religious activity, including prayer.

The legal rules that govern the issue of constitutionally protected prayer in the public schools are similar to those that govern religious expression generally. Thus, in discussing the operation of Section 9524 of the ESEA, this guidance sometimes speaks in terms of "religious expression." There are a variety of issues relating to religion in the public schools, however, that this guidance is not intended to address.

The Supreme Court has repeatedly held that the First Amendment requires public school officials to be neutral in their treatment of religion, showing neither favoritism toward nor hostility against religious expression such as prayer. (2) Accordingly, the First Amendment forbids religious activity that is sponsored by the government but protects religious activity that is initiated by private individuals, and the line between government-sponsored and privately initiated religious expression is vital to a proper understanding of the First Amendment's scope. As the Court has explained in several cases, "there is a crucial difference between government speech endorsing religion, which the Establishment Clause forbids, and private speech endorsing religion, which the Free Speech and Free Exercise Clauses protect." (3)

The Supreme Court's decisions over the past forty years set forth principles that distinguish impermissible governmental religious speech from the constitutionally protected private religious speech of students. For example, teachers and other public school officials may not lead their classes in prayer, devotional readings from the Bible, or other religious activities.(4) Nor may school officials attempt to persuade or compel students to participate in prayer or other religious activities. (5) Such conduct is "attributable to the State" and thus violates the Establishment Clause. (6)

Similarly, public school officials may not themselves decide that prayer should be included in school-sponsored events. In Lee v. Weisman (7), for example, the Supreme Court held that public school officials violated the Constitution in inviting a member of the clergy to deliver a prayer at a graduation ceremony. Nor may school officials grant religious speakers preferential access to public audiences, or otherwise select public speakers on a basis that favors religious speech. In Santa Fe Independent School District v. Doe (8), for example, the Court invalidated a school's football game speaker policy on the ground that it was designed by school officials to result in pregame prayer, thus favoring religious expression over secular expression.

Although the Constitution forbids public school officials from directing or favoring prayer, students do not "shed their constitutional rights to freedom of speech or expression at the schoolhouse gate," (9) and the Supreme Court has made clear that "private religious speech, far from being a First Amendment orphan, is as fully protected under the Free Speech Clause as secular private expression." (10) Moreover, not all religious speech that takes place in the public schools or at school-sponsored events is governmental speech. (11) For example, "nothing in the Constitution ... prohibits any public school student from voluntarily praying at any time before, during, or after the school day," (12) and students may pray with fellow students during the school day on the same terms and conditions that they may engage in other conversation or speech. Likewise, local school authorities possess substantial discretion to impose rules of order and pedagogical restrictions on student activities, (13) but they may not structure or administer such rules to discriminate against student prayer or religious speech. For instance, where schools permit student expression on the basis of genuinely neutral criteria and students retain primary control over the content of their expression, the speech of students who choose to express themselves through religious means such as prayer is not attributable to the state and therefore may not be restricted because of its religious content. (14) Student remarks are not attributable to the state simply because they are delivered in a public setting or to a public audience. (15) As the Supreme Court has explained: "The proposition that schools do not endorse everything they fail to censor is not complicated," (16) and the Constitution mandates neutrality rather than hostility toward privately initiated religious expression. (17)

Applying the Governing Principles in Particular Contexts: Prayer during Non-instructional Time:

Students may pray when not engaged in school activities or instruction, subject to the same rules designed to prevent material disruption of the educational program that are applied to other privately initiated expressive activities. Among other things, students may read their Bibles or other scriptures, say grace before meals, and pray or study religious materials with fellow students during recess, the lunch hour, or other non-instructional time to the same extent that they may engage in nonreligious activities. While school authorities may impose rules of order and pedagogical restrictions on student activities, they may not discriminate against student prayer or religious speech in applying such rules and restrictions.

Organized Prayer Groups and Activities:

Students may organize prayer groups, religious clubs, and "see you at the pole" gatherings before school to the same extent that students are permitted to organize other non-curricular student activities groups. Such groups must be given the same access to school facilities for assembling as is given to other non-curricular groups, without discrimination because of the religious content of their expression. School authorities possess substantial discretion concerning whether to permit the use of school media for student advertising or announcements regarding non-curricular activities. However, where student groups that meet for nonreligious activities are permitted to advertise or announce their meetings-for example, by advertising in a student newspaper, making announcements on a student activities bulletin board or public address system, or handing out leaflets-school authorities may not discriminate against groups who meet to pray. School authorities may disclaim sponsorship of non-curricular groups and events, provided they administer such disclaimers in a manner that neither favors nor disfavors groups that meet to engage in prayer or religious speech.

Teachers, Administrators, and other School Employees:

When acting in their official capacities as representatives of the state, teachers, school administrators, and other school employees are prohibited by the Establishment Clause from encouraging or discouraging prayer, and from actively participating in such activity with students. Teachers may, however, take part in religious activities where the overall context makes clear that they are not participating in their official capacities. Before school or during lunch, for example, teachers may meet with other teachers for prayer or Bible study to the same extent that they may engage in other conversation or nonreligious activities. Similarly, teachers may participate in their personal capacities in privately sponsored baccalaureate ceremonies.

Moments of Silence:

If a school has a "minute of silence" or other quiet periods during the school day, students are free to pray silently, or not to pray, during these periods of time. Teachers and other school employees may neither encourage nor discourage students from praying during such time periods.

Accommodation of Prayer during Instructional Time:

It has long been established that schools have the discretion to dismiss students to off-premises religious instruction, provided that schools do not encourage or discourage participation in such instruction or penalize students for attending or not attending. Similarly, schools may excuse students from class to remove a significant burden on their religious exercise, where doing so would not impose material burdens on other students. For example, it would be lawful for schools to excuse Muslim students briefly from class to enable them to fulfill their religious obligations to pray during Ramadan.

Where school officials have a practice of excusing students from class on the basis of parents' requests for accommodation of nonreligious needs, religiously motivated requests for excusal may not be accorded less favorable treatment. In addition, in some circumstances, based on federal or state constitutional law or pursuant to state statutes, schools may be required to make accommodations that relieve substantial burdens on students' religious exercise. School officials are therefore encouraged to consult with their attorneys regarding such obligations

Religious Expression and Prayer in Class Assignments:

Students may express their beliefs about religion in homework, artwork, and other written and oral assignments free from discrimination based on the religious content of their submissions. Such home and classroom work should be judged by ordinary academic standards of substance and relevance and against other legitimate pedagogical concerns identified by the school. Thus, if a teacher's assignment involves writing a poem, the work of a student who submits a poem in the form of a prayer (for example, a psalm) should be judged on the basis of academic standards (such as literary quality) and neither penalized nor rewarded on account of its religious content.

Student Assemblies and Extracurricular Events:

Student speakers at student assemblies and extracurricular activities such

151

as sporting events may not be selected on a basis that either favors or disfavors religious speech. Where student speakers are selected on the basis of genuinely neutral, evenhanded criteria and retain primary control over the content of their expression, that expression is not attributable to the school and therefore may not be restricted because of its religious (or anti-religious) content. By contrast, where school officials determine or substantially control the content of what is expressed, such speech is attributable to the school and may not include prayer or other specifically religious (or anti-religious) content. To avoid any mistaken perception that a school endorses student speech that is not in fact attributable to the school, school officials may make appropriate, neutral disclaimers to clarify that such speech (whether religious or nonreligious) is the speaker's and not the school's.

Prayer at Graduation:

School officials may not mandate or organize prayer at graduation or select speakers for such events in a manner that favors religious speech such as prayer. Where students or other private graduation speakers are selected on the basis of genuinely neutral, evenhanded criteria and retain primary control over the content of their expression, however, that expression is not attributable to the school and therefore may not be restricted because of its religious (or anti-religious) content. To avoid any mistaken perception that a school endorses student or other private speech that is not in fact attributable to the school, school officials may make appropriate, neutral disclaimers to clarify that such speech (whether religious or nonreligious) is the speaker's and not the school's.

Baccalaureate Ceremonies:

School officials may not mandate or organize religious ceremonies. However, if a school makes its facilities and related services available to other private groups, it must make its facilities and services available on the same terms to organizers of privately sponsored religious baccalaureate ceremonies. In addition, a school may disclaim official endorsement of events sponsored by private groups, provided it does so in a manner that neither favors nor disfavors groups that meet to engage in prayer or religious speech.

Notes:

[1] The relevant portions of the First Amendment provide: "Congress shall make no law respecting an establishment of religion, or prohibiting the free exercise thereof; or abridging the freedom of speech . . . ." U.S. Const. Amend. I. The Supreme Court has held that the Fourteenth Amendment makes these

provisions applicable to all levels of government-federal, state, and local-and to all types of governmental policies and activities. See Everson v. Board of Educ., 330 U.S. 1 (1947); Cantwell v. Connecticut, 310 U.S. 296 (1940).

[2] See, e.g., Everson, 330 U.S. at 18 (the First Amendment "requires the state to be a neutral in its relations with groups of religious believers and non-believers; it does not require the state to be their adversary. State power is no more to be used so as to handicap religions than it is to favor them"); Good News Club v. Milford Cent. Sch., 533 U.S. 98 (2001).

[3] Santa Fe Indep. Sch. Dist. v. Doe, 530 U.S. 290, 302 (2000) (quoting Board of Educ. v. Mergens, 496 U.S. 226, 250 (1990) (plurality opinion)); accord Rosenberger v. Rector of Univ. of Virginia, 515 U.S. 819, 841 (1995).

[4] Engel v. Vitale, 370 U.S. 421 (1962) (invalidating state laws directing the use of prayer in public schools); School Dist. of Abington Twp. v. Schempp, 374 U.S. 203 (1963) (invalidating state laws and policies requiring public schools to begin the school day with Bible readings and prayer); Mergens, 496 U.S. at 252 (plurality opinion) (explaining that "a school may not itself lead or direct a religious club"). The Supreme Court has also held, however, that the study of the Bible or of religion, when presented objectively as part of a secular program of education (e.g., in history or literature classes), is consistent with the First Amendment. See Schempp, 374 U.S. at 225.

[5] See Lee v. Weisman, 505 U.S. 577, 599 (1992); see also Wallace v. Jaffree, 472 U.S. 38 (1985).

[6] See Weisman, 505 U.S. at 587.

[7] 505 U.S. 577 (1992).

[8] 530 U.S. 290 (2000).

[9] Tinker v. Des Moines Indep. Community Sch. Dist., 393 U.S. 503, 506 (1969).

[10] Capitol Square Review & Advisory Bd. v. Pinette, 515 U.S. 753, 760 (1995).

[11] Santa Fe, 530 U.S. at 302 (explaining that "not every message" that is

"authorized by a government policy and take[s] place on government property at government-sponsored school-related events" is "the government's own").

[12] Santa Fe, 530 U.S. at 313.

[13] For example, the First Amendment permits public school officials to review student speeches for vulgarity, lewdness, or sexually explicit language. Bethel Sch. Dist. v. Fraser, 478 U.S. 675, 683-86 (1986). Without more, however, such review does not make student speech attributable to the state.

[14] Rosenberger v. Rector of Univ. of Virginia, 515 U.S. 819 (1995); Board of Educ. v. Mergens, 496 U.S. 226 (1990); Good News Club v. Milford Cent. Sch., 533 U.S. 98 (2001); Lamb's Chapel v. Center Moriches Union Free Sch. Dist., 508 U.S. 384 (1993); Widmar v. Vincent, 454 U.S. 263 (1981); Santa Fe, 530 U.S. at 304 n.15. In addition, in circumstances where students are entitled to pray, public schools may not restrict or censor their prayers on the ground that they might be deemed "too religious" to others. The Establishment Clause prohibits state officials from making judgments about what constitutes an appropriate prayer, and from favoring or disfavoring certain types of prayers-be they "nonsectarian" and "nonproselytizing" or the opposite-over others. See Engel v. Vitale, 370 U.S. 421, 429-30 (1962) (explaining that "one of the greatest dangers to the freedom of the individual to worship in his own way lay in the Government's placing its official stamp of approval upon one particular kind of prayer or one particular form of religious services," that "neither the power nor the prestige" of state officials may "be used to control, support or influence the kinds of prayer the American people can say," and that the state is "without power to prescribe by law any particular form of prayer"); Weisman, 505 U.S. at 594.

[15] Santa Fe, 530 U.S. at 302; Mergens, 496 U.S. at 248-50.

[16] Mergens, 496 U.S. at 250 (plurality opinion); id. at 260-61 (Kennedy, J., concurring in part and in judgment).

[17] Rosenberger, 515 U.S. at 845-46; Mergens, 496 U.S. at 248 (plurality opinion); id. at 260-61 (Kennedy, J., concurring in part and in judgment).

APPENDIX 6
Website Resource List

Association of American Educators
www.aaeteachers.org

Association of Christian Schools International (ACSI)
www.acsi.org

Bible Education in School Time (BEST)
www.bestnetwork.org

Billy Graham Evangelistic Association
www.billygraham.org

California Released Time Christian Education Association (CRT-CEA)
www.califreleasedtime.org

California School Project
www.californiaschoolproject.com

Campus Crusade for Christ
www.campuscrusade.org

Child Evangelism Fellowship
www.cefonline.com

Christ in Youth
www.ciy.com

Christian Educators Association International
www.ceai.org

Concerned Women for America
www.cwfa.org

Eagle Forum
www.eagleforum.org

Exodus International
www.exodusinternational.org

Fellowship and Christian Encouragement (FACE) for Educators
www.prayingeducator.org

Fellowship of Christian Athletes (FCA)
www.fca.org

Fellowship of Christian Release Time Ministries (FCRTM)
www.rtce.org

Focus On The Family
www.family.org

Love Won Out
www.lovewonout.com

National Coalition for the Protection of Children & Families
www.nationalcoalition.org

National Council on Bible Curriculum in Public Schools
www.bibleinschools.net

National Day of Prayer
www.nationaldayofprayer.org

Gateways to Better Education
www.gtbe.com

Harvest Crusade
www.harvest.org

Miles Ahead Ministries
www.milesahead.com

Moms in Touch Ministries
www.momsintouch.org

One Kid At A Time Inc.
www.onekidatatime.org

Summit Ministries
www.summit.org

Wallbuilders
www.wallbuilders.org

Young Life
www.younglife.org

Youth for Christ
www.yfc.org

Youth Specialties
www.youthspecialties.com

END NOTES

Introduction

[1] 2 Timothy 1:7 (New International Version).

[2] 1 Peter 3:15 (New International Version).

[3] 2 Timothy 1:8 (New International Version).

[4] 2 Corinthians 5:14-15 (New American Standard Version).

[5] Charles Sheldon, In His Steps (New Jersey: Barbour & Company, Inc., 1985), 238.

Chapter 1 – Are You Ready?

[6] Joshua 1:9 (New International Version).

Chapter 2 – Truth Be Told

[7] Dobson/Bauer, *Children At Risk* (Dallas: Word Publishing, 1990), 250-251.

[8] *Lynch v. Donnelly*, 465 U.S. 668 (1981).

[9] See Appendix 3 for a statement regarding equal access that was endorsed by a wide breadth of organizations ranging from the CLS (Christian Legal Society) to the ACLU (American Civil Liberties Union), and signed as an Administrative Directive by former President William J. Clinton.

Chapter 3– I Dare You To Ask Me About Jesus

[10] *Good News/Good Sports Club v. Milford Central School*, 533 U.S. 98 (2001).

[11] 20 U.S.C. § 4071.

[12] *Garnett v. Renton SD*, 772 F. Supp. 531 (W.D. Wash 1991), reversed by *Garnett v. Renton School District*, 987 F.2 641 (9th Cir. 1993) [state law superceded by the federal Equal Access Act].

¹³ *Van Schoick v. Saddleback Valley Unified School District,* 87 Cal. App 4th 522 (2001).

¹⁴ *Ceniceros v. San Diego Unified School District,* 106 F.3d 878 (9th Cir. 1997).

¹⁵ *Good News/Good Sports Club v. School District of Ladue,* 28 F.3d 1501 (8th Cir. 1994). See also Good News Club, and *Culbertson v. Oakridge* District, No. 76 , 258 F.3d 1061 (9th Cir. 2001).

¹⁶ For a definitive court decision discussing the free speech rights of students see *Tinker v. Des Moines Independent Community School District,* 393 U.S. 503 (1969).

¹⁷ The Establishment Clause of the U.S. Constitution's First Amendment generally forbids government hostility to religion. See Lynch, supra note 8 at 673.

¹⁸ *Harper v. Poway Unified School District,* 455 F.3d 1052 (9th Cir. 2006)

¹⁹ *Lee v. Weisman,* 505 U.S. 577 (1992).

²⁰ *Cole v. Oroville Union High School District,* 228 F.3d 1092(9th Cir. 2000)

²¹ *Adler v. Duval County School Board,* 250 F.3d. 1330 (11th Cir. 2001).

²² *Adler v. Duval County School Board,* 122 S. Ct. 664 (2001).

²³ See Adler, supra n.21 and *Jones v. Clear Creek Independent School District,* 977 F.2d 963 (5th Cir. 1992)

²⁴ 530 U.S. 290 (2000).

²⁵ See Id. at 317.

²⁶ In Tinker, supra note 16, the Supreme Court upheld restrictions on student speech: 1) where the expressive activity materially disrupts the educa-

tional process; or 2) where the expressive activity "colli[des] with the rights of other students to be secure and to be let alone."

[27] *Heffron v. International Society of Krishna Consciousness*, 452 US 640 (1981); *Hedges v. Wauconda Community Unit School Dist. No. 118*, 9 F.3d 1295 (7th Cir 1993)

[28] *Tinker v. Des Moines Independent Community School District*, 393 U.S. 503 (1969).

[29] *Doe v. Duncanville Independent School District.*, 70 F.3d 402 (5th Cir. 1995).

[30] *Santa Fe Independent School District v. Doe*, 120 S. Ct. 2266, 2281 (2000).

[31] *Tinker v. Des Moines Independent Community School District*, 393 U.S. 503 (1969).

[32] *Daugherty v. Vanguard Charter Academy*, 116 F. Supp. 2d 897, 910 (W.D. Mich. 2000))

Chapter 4 – The High Calling of a Teacher

[33] *Breen v. Runkel*, 614 F.Supp. 355 (D.C. Mich. 1985).

[34] In *Texas State Teachers Association v. Garland Independent School District*, 777 F.2d 1046 (5th Cir. 1985), a federal court of appeals concluded that teachers have more freedom to share their faith during "contract time" (verses "classroom time"). In addition, a teacher discussing religion with students during "contract time" does not involve the "captive student audience" inherent with "classroom time" instruction.

[35] *Peloza v. Capistrano Unified School District*, 37 F3d 517 (9th Cir. 1994).

[36] Howard O. Hunter, Curriculum, Pedagogy, and the Constitutional Rights of teachers in Secondary Schools, 25 Wm. & Mary L. Rev. 1 (1983).

[37] *Peloza v. Capistrano Unified School District*, supra note 35

[38] *McLean v. Arkansas Board of Education*, 529 F.Supp. 1255, 1264-66 (E.D.Ark. 1982).

[39] *Florey v. Sioux Falls School District* 49-5, 464 F. Supp. 911 (D.S.D. 1980), affirmed by *Florey v. Sioux Falls School District* 619 F.2d 1311 (8th Cir. 1980); See also Duncanville, supra note 29, at 407.

[40] The Establishment Clause and its Application in the Public Schools, 59 Neb. L. Rev. 1143 (1980).

[41] *Pickering v. Board of Education*, 391 U.S. 563 (1968); See also *Mt. Healthy City School District Bd. Of Educ. v. Doyle*, 429 U.S. 274 (1977).

[42] *Santa Fe I.S.D. v. Jane Doe*, 530 U.S. 290 (2000)

[43] See *Freethought Society v. Chester County*, 334 F.3d 247 (3d Cir. 2003); Cf. *Indiana ACLU v. O'Bannon*, 259 F.3d 766 (7th Cir. 2001) [accompanying Bill of Rights monument was deemed to be too small to be noticed when seen with proposed Ten Commandments monument].

[44] *CWA v. Beck*, 487 U.S. 735 (1988).

[45] 42 USCS 2000e (2004))

[46] *Int'l Assn. Of Machinists v. Boeing*, 833 F.2d 165, 169 (9th Cir. 1987) and *Wilson v. NLRB*, 920 F.2d 1282 (6th Cir. 1990).

[47] The employee may, however, be required to produce some sort of independent corroboration to support his/her sincere religious beliefs claim. Such corroboration need not come from a pastor or other church official. See *Bushouse v. Local Union 2209*, 164 F.Supp.2d 1066 (N.D. Ind. 2001).

Chapter 5– What's A Church To Do?

[48] *Illinois ex rel. McCollum v. Board of Education*, 333 U.S. 203 (1948); *Zorach v. Clauson*, 343 U.S. 306 (1952).

[49] *Peek v. Upshur County Board of Education*, 155 F.3d 274 (4th Cir. 1998)

[50] *Fairfax Covenant Church v. Fairfax C.S.B.*, 17 F.3d 703 (4th Cir. 1994).

[51] Good News Club, supra note 10.

[52] Id.

Chapter 6– But I'm Just a Parent

[53] *Pierce v. Society of Sisters*, 268 U.S. 510(1925).

[54] *Brown v. Woodland Joint Unified School District*, 27 F.3d 1373 (9th Cir. 1994).

[55] 20 U.S.C. § 1232h. (See Appendix 4).

[56] Deuteronomy (New International Version).

Chapter 7 – What's a School TO Do?

[57] Larry Caldwell, Attorney at Law (Inner quotes from California State Board of Education Policy on the Teaching of Natural Sciences – 1989)

[58] *Adler v. Duval County*, 250 F.3d 1330 (11th Cir. 2001)

[59] Title 42 USC Section 2000 e-2 (701j of Title VII)

Chapter 8– What if I Don't Remember

[60] James 1:17 (New International Version).

[61] Hebrews 10:25 (New International Version).

[62] Romans 10:14 (New International Version) (Bold added).